Guy
Kawasaki

THE

Computer
Curmudgeon

HAYDEN

The Computer Curmudgeon

Copyright © 1992 by Guy Kawasaki.

Library of Congress Catalog No.: 92-074870

ISBN: 1-56830-013-1

94   93   92   4   3   2   1

Interpretation of the printing code: the rightmost double-digit number is the year of the book's printing; the rightmost single-digit number is the number of the book's printing. For example, a printing code of 92-1 shows that the first printing of the book occurred in 1992.

The Computer Curmudgeon is the first in a four-book series by Guy Kawasaki. Look for the next three titles:

The MS-DOS Curmudgeon

The Windows Curmudgeon

The UNIX Curmudgeon

And if you believe that, you're not the target market of the book, so put it back and save your shekels.

Credits

Publisher   Mike Britton

Project Manager   Karen Whitehouse

Development Editor   Dave Ciskowski

Designer   Scott Cook

Illustrator   John Ceballos

Production Team   Katy Bodenmiller, Christine Cook, Tim Cox, Mark Enochs, Tim Groeling, Phil Kitchel, Jay Lesandrini, Tom Loveman, Carrie Roth, Michelle Self, Susan Shepherd, Kelli Widdifield

Composed in ITC Garamond, Helvetica, and MCPdigital by Hayden.

Dedication

To my wife Beth, without whom there would be no humor in my life.

To Jon Winokur, who inspired this book with *The Portable Curmudgeon*.

To Apple employees—past, present, and future—who created, are creating, and will create insanely great computers.

About the Author

Guy Kawasaki

Guy Kawasaki is the former director of software product management for Apple Computer, Inc. In this position, he cajoled, coerced, and convinced software and hardware companies to create products for a computer that didn't have enough RAM, a hard disk, color, slots, an installed base, technical support, or marketing.

He has a BA from Stanford in Psychology ("the easiest major I could find") and an MBA from UCLA ("because Stanford rejected me"). While he waits for the Golden State Warriors to call him, he writes, speaks, and promotes products ("I endorse, therefore I am").

Trademark Acknowledgments

There are too many trademark acknowledgments to list on this page. Because we are environmentalists, and because paper is a valuable (and therefore costly) commodity, we will limit our trademark acknowledgments to the following statement:

All terms in this book that are known to be trademarks or service marks have been appropriately capitalized. Hayden cannot attest to the accuracy of this information. Use of a term in this book should not be regarded as affecting the validity of any trademark or service mark.

We Want to Hear from You

What our readers think of Hayden is crucial to our sense of well-being. If you have any comments, no matter how great or how small, we'd appreciate your taking the time to send us a note, using any of the several methods provided for your convenience.

Mike Britton
Hayden Books
11711 North College Avenue
Carmel, IN 46032
(317) 573-2583 fax

E-mail addresses:
AppleLink: haydenbks.mb
CompuServe: 76350,3014
America Online: MikeHayden

Acknowledgments

Creating a book is a team effort. It takes a publisher, editors, artists, designers, proofreaders, production people, and beta testers. And a writer. Here's *The Computer Curmudgeon* Team:

The Inside Team

Mike Britton. Mike was my evangelist at Hayden. He caught the vision and fought the doubters to take Hayden where it has never gone before.

Dave Ciskowski. Dave developed this book, content- and copy-edited it, coordinated the actions of the Hayden team, and bore the brunt of my incessant badgering.

Karen Whitehouse. Karen was the "iron fist inside the velvet glove" that kept the book going. She even helped with my next book.

Scott Cook. Scott designed the book and was instrumental in taking care of the hundreds of questions that arose. Without his efforts, the book would not have been finished in the astoundingly short period it was.

Kathy Hanley, Marj Hopper, Mat Wahlstrom, Laura Wirthlin, Michael Nolan, and Jay Corpus. They designed, suggested, illustrated, and massaged the book into reality.

Mark my words: Hayden will be a force in computer books.

The Outside Team

Henry Berger, Andrew Carol, Matt Evens, Patrick Fox, John Holland, Julius Sarkozy, Alan Spurgeon, Robin Williams, and Richard Wolpert. They made suggestions and contributions that vastly improved the book.

Donald Daybell. Donald contributed *The Unofficial Smilie Dictionary*. By compiling and supplementing this dictionary, he helped E-mail addicts all over the world.

John Ceballos. John illustrated this book. With nothing more than a few phrases, he was able to understand the essence of the book and create the cover and illustrations.

John Michel. John works for Harmony Books. He couldn't get Harmony to publish the book, but he kept me psyched as I was writing it. Someday I wish he would *publish* a book of mine...

Foreword

If Mark Twain were alive today he might have written this book.

To be accurate, if Mark Twain were alive today, he'd be scratching on the lid of his coffin, screaming for help.

I guess what I mean is that if Mark Twain were a Twentieth century Chicklet-toothed techno-samurai with the energy of a caffeinated ferret and the timidity of an armed Jehovah's witness, he might have written this book.

Of course, then Huck Finn would have rafted down the Sacramento River, teaching Jim about "da innerface."

One day Guy Kawasaki will finally say everything he can possibly say about the human/computer experience. Eighty-seven articles and three books later he will stop writing.

I miss him already.

Harry Anderson
Magician, TV Personality, and Mac User

Introduction

After some failure and some success in business, I've come to believe that the First Rule of Business is: "Under-promise and over-deliver."

(When convenient) I like to practice what I preach, so here goes:

The sole purpose of *The Computer Curmudgeon* is to make you laugh.

That's it. Nothing more, nothing less.

This book will not provide insights into paradigm-shifting, enterprise-wide, cross-platform, money-minting megatrends for the '90s.

It will, however, upset a lot of people. Mostly rich, powerful, hypocritical wimps. And PC owners.

Frankly, I've come to believe the Second Rule of Business is: "You measure your worth, not by who likes you, but by who dislikes you."

I am very proud of who dislikes me. I hope this book makes them dislike me even more and garners new dislikers too.

More than anything else, I hope this book will make you laugh because then I have done my job: bringing some humor into your life.

Guy Kawasaki
San Francisco, The City, the Bay Area—
anything but "Frisco"—California

October, 1992

Guide to the Use of this Book

This book has four components:

- Definitions. Definitions appear in alphabetical order and are set in boldface extending slightly into the left margin.

  Apple marketing The largest group of migrant workers in California.

- Rules of thumb. Rules of thumb appear after the definition they pertain to. They are set in italic type.

  COMDEX 100,000 people trying to find a cab.

  The first indication that a Macintosh software company is going down the toilet is exhibiting at COMDEX.

- Column reprints. Column reprints appear at the end of the chapter that contains the definition they pertain to.

  The column reprints were selected for their timelessness—that is, remaining pertinent and useful no matter when they were originally published.

- Top X lists and other miscellaneous stuff. These lists and writings appear after the definition they pertain to.

More on Silicon Valley...

The Five Best License Plates In Silicon Valley

5.	Bill Gates	COPY MAC
4.	John Sculley	SUE BILL
3.	Steve Jobs	NO SFTWR
2.	Jean-Louis Gassée	GRN CARD
1.	Beth Kawasaki	NO EMAIL

If You Want to Write

I love to hear from people who have read my books. Please contact me at:

Guy Kawasaki
P.O. Box 471090
San Francisco, CA 94107-1090

Fax: 415-921-2479
AppleLink: Kawasaki2
CompuServe: 76703,3031
America Online: Mac Way
Internet: MacWay@AOL.Com (Please, only as a last resort!) ;-)

The modern definition of curmudgeon, according to the curmudgeon's curmudgeon, Jon Winokur, is

"Anyone who hates hypocrisy and pretense and has the temerity to say so; anyone with the habit of pointing out unpleasant facts in an engaging and humorous manner."

Apple Proof that as long as your customers are still complaining, they're still willing to do business with you.

about box The principal goal for Macintosh programmers—that is, getting their names in it.[1]

accelerator A hardware device that makes your Macintosh run just as fast as the Macintosh just discontinued by Apple.

---

[1] Thanks to Andrew Carol.

access time   The length of time it takes to get through a voice-mail system to talk to a human.

> *Always leave your phone number on a voice-mail message—no matter how many times you've called the person before. (The person you called may retrieve your message from an airport or a car and not have your number handy.)*

ACIUS   Apple Computer Incorporated Unshipped Software.

active matrix display   Computer displays whose non-existent U.S. manufacturers the U.S. government protects.

ADB   Apple-DEC Bust. See also *alliance*.

AFM   Adobe Fooled Microsoft.

After Dark   Proof that Macintosh owners have too much money.

alias   "MBA" for "bozo."

alliance   The temporary union of organizations whose executives think they have mutual or overlapping goals.

> *An "alliance" becomes a "strategic alliance" when losing money becomes inevitable.*

> *No alliance lasts more than two years or the vesting period of the executives that formed it—whichever is less.*

alpha version   Software that helps a company get a second round of venture capital.

amazed What Macintosh owners are when Airborne Express comes to pick up their PowerBook for a free, two-day repair.

analog Anything easy to read in direct sunlight.

ANSI A standard, but in a fidgety sort of way.[2]

APDA Attempt Programming During Adolescence.

Apollo The god of workstations.

Apple Proof that as long as your customers are still complaining, they're still willing to do business with you.

> *Apple will discontinue the model of Macintosh you bought within three months of your purchase.*
>
> *If you don't like an Apple policy, wait six months, and it will change.*
>
> *If you like an Apple policy, wait six months, and it will change.*

For still more on Apple, see "From The Desk Of," at the end of this chapter.

Apple consultant The product of a technique designed to increase sales volume per employee while sacrificing the bottom line.

> *Laid-off Apple employees return to Apple as consultants and make three times more money.*

Apple management The unqualified, doing the unnecessary, for the unappreciative. See also *oxymoron*.

"Apple will discontinue the model of Macintosh you bought within three months of your purchase."

---

[2] Thanks to Andrew Carol.

Apple marketing   The largest group of migrant workers in California.

> *Q. What's the difference between Apple and the Boy Scouts?*
>
> *A. The Boy Scouts have adult supervision.*

AppleLink   A marketing research project to determine whether people will pay $25/hour for electronic mail service when $5/hour services are available.

> *America Online is for geeks; CompuServe is for tweaks; AppleLink is for sheiks; The Well is for freaks.*

AppleTalk   "Strategic," "integrated," "focused," "enterprise-wide," "alliance."

application   Doing in 1400K what can be done in 200K. See also *desk accessory*.

archive   A collection of files you should have thrown away.

artificial intelligence   Whatever it takes to get a venture capitalist to invest in your company.

ascender   An MBA on the rise.

ATM   Adobe Tricked Microsoft.

authorized Apple dealer   A store that doesn't provide service and support but charges for them. See also *superstore*.

"America Online is for geeks; CompuServe is for tweaks; AppleLink is for sheiks; The Well is for freaks."

More on authorized Apple dealers...

The Four Best Things Heard in the Computer Department of the UCLA Bookstore[3]

4. "My disky flops don't work."

3. "Do you sell the Apple II SE/30?"

2. "Do you sell Windows for Macintosh?"

1. "The screen on my Macintosh Plus won't come on. It probably needs a new bulb."

More on Apple...

From the Desk of

Reprinted from *MacUser* December 1991

The personal-computer business is in a panic these days because of slower sales growth, lower margins, and general uneasiness about where the industry and the economy are headed. In light of this, two of the sharpest people in software—Bill Gates, of Microsoft, and John Walker, of Autodesk—have written internal memos about the challenges and issues their respective companies face. Also, an employee of IBM recently supposedly posted some of the harsh remarks that CEO John Akers had to say at an IBM managers' meeting about IBM's performance.

[3] Thanks to Henry Berger.

The two documents and Akers' remarks got a great deal of press. I guess it's hip these days to communicate bad news and potential threats to employees—thereby scaring them into greater efforts. I've waited for Apple to do this, but it hasn't been forthcoming. Thus, I've decided to do it for Apple. (If I can't be on the board, I might as well try to be the CEO.)

My Fellow Apple Employees:

As we enter the first quarter of fiscal year 1992, it is appropriate and important to discuss the issues and challenges Apple faces in the coming year. My purpose is not to frighten or alarm you. Rather, I seek to communicate my thoughts so that we may go forward with one purpose and one resolve.

I've divided the most important issues and challenges into three categories.

Category 1 This category contains issues that we control and are therefore entirely responsible for dealing with. Frankly, we can hurt ourselves more than most external forces such as competitors and the national economy can hurt us.

- **Leapfrog Macintosh.** Our greatest technical challenge is creating a computer that leapfrogs Macintosh just as Macintosh leapfrogged the IBM PC (and the Apple IIe—but it's not politically correct for me to say that). In the next five to seven years, Macintosh technology will reach the end of its lifetime, and if we don't cannibalize Macintosh sales, someone else will. Nothing is more important to the long-term viability of Apple than accomplishing this goal.

More on Apple...

- **Customer support.** Championship teams have both a great offense and a great defense. Our offense must create world-class innovative products. Our defense must provide world-class empathetic customer support. We have taken positive steps, such as our 800 and System 7 telephone lines, to improve customer support, but this isn't enough. Apple's customers express surprise when they receive support; Nordstrom's customers express surprise when they don't. We should be the Nordstrom of the personal-computer industry. This is the responsibility of Apple employees every time they come into contact with the public.

- **Corporate bulimia nervosa.** Our binge-and-purge hiring practices must end. We're not building a stable management structure, and employees seem more concerned with saving their skin than changing the world. If we need to, we will take short-term earnings hits in order to keep our people. We will also cut back on the perks and luxuries of working at Apple so we can afford to keep people. In the long run, a stable workforce will lead to greater earnings and higher stock prices.

- **Bozo explosion.** Given a commitment to long-term employment, we must carefully scrutinize who we are hiring, because new employees will be with us for a long time. In the past, we've used lower earnings projections to justify laying off bozos and have had less fear of lawsuits. We won't be able to do this anymore. When we hire people, we must remember that only two things matter: their ability to perform in the position and their love of personal computers. I encourage you to look beyond paper qualifications such as educational back-ground and work experience. Let's draft the best athletes, not hire "has-been's" who "have done it before" somewhere else.

Category 2 This category contains issues that involve external constituencies. Although we do not solely control these relationships, I believe that we can conduct our affairs much better.

- **Third-party developers.** Third-party develop-ers provide the reason to buy our computers. In the past few years, unfortunately, we seem to have forgotten our friends. Because of budget cutbacks, for example, we've concentrated on several hundred developers (the "A list"). Some of the most innovative and loyal developers, however, are not on the A list, and they are being shuffled to the side. The two most important attributes of our third-party developers are product quality and loyalty to our products. Size, brand name aware-ness, and how much an industry analyst likes a company should be inconsequential.

- **Early adopters.** When Apple stands tall, it's be-cause it has one foot on a shoulder of third-party developers and the other foot on a shoulder of our early adopters. Early adopters are the people who bought an Apple II and a Macintosh 128K and who have been with us for years. These people are the roots of Apple, so let us not be seduced by big numbers in business and forget our loyal fans. Remember that when we introduce the computer that leapfrogs Macintosh, these will be the first people to step up to the plate while big business hems and haws about installed base, backward compatibility, and their "investment" in Macintosh.

- **Loving Microsoft (to death).** Let me make one thing perfectly clear: Microsoft is one of our most dangerous threats. The best scenario for our relationship with Microsoft is détente, not alliance. We should unabashedly promote Microsoft and its products only if and when it unabashedly helps us sell more Macintoshes. The key to our Microsoft strategy is recognizing that Microsoft can furnish key applications and signal acceptability of Macintosh until other developers produce better products. Let's not be naive about what's going on. Let's think of Microsoft as a mighty opposite: If we can control or defeat Microsoft, we can dominate the personal-computer industry.

- **The IBM Alliance.** Our newly-formed relationship with IBM is an important step to achieving legitimacy in the business market. (I hope you don't think that we really care about IBM's technology.) We should capitalize on this relationship when people doubt our products' desirability: "If it's GUI enough for IBM, it's GUI enough for you." The IBM relationship, however, is not a guarantee of success or a panacea. IBM is looking out for IBM; Apple is looking out for Apple. Sometimes our goals may overlap. Sometimes they won't. At all times, we are responsible for our own fate. IBM walked away from Rolm; it will certainly walk away from our alliance when it's advantageous.

- **Crisis in the computer-store channel.** Jean-Louis Gassée used to say that Apple should do what's right for customers and that then all the other pieces will fall into place. One thing we've done right is recognize that people want to buy our products in a no-frills, economical way, and thus we've authorized superstores as Apple resellers. Our goal is not to create a crisis in the computer-store channel, but to do what's right for our customer. Frankly, the crisis may indicate that computer stores have not provided the value for which customers are willing to pay. Our position will be to support both computer stores and superstores and let customers decide where to buy their Apple products.

Category 3 This category contains issues that are not widely recognized or perhaps have been incorrectly dismissed.

- **NeXT.** We should not take the competitive threat of NeXT and Steve Jobs lightly. His computer offers a very attractive price/performance ratio that competes directly with the high end of our product line. All his talk about "professional workstations" is just a smoke screen until he has the software and buying and production capacity to produce a "personal computer." Steve, no matter what he publicly professes, wants to create three of the four personal-computer standards. Eventually he wants to own it all.

- **Sony.** We are one of Sony's biggest customers, and Sony has worked with us in the design of one of our new computers. Neither of these facts, however, should cloud the fact that Sony could be a formidable competitor in the personal-computer market if it ever decided to enter it. Sony, frankly, is one of the few companies that could acquire Apple and successfully operate it after the acquisition has occurred—to wit, Sony's handling of CBS Records has been exemplary. Let's keep our eyes open when we deal with the slant-eyed devils from the East.

Thank you very much for reading this memo. If you have comments about it, please contact me on AppleLink. I look forward to a bright future for Apple and all its employees.

Sincerely,
Guy Kawasaki,
Self-anointed CEO

(By the way, when I worked for Apple I always hated it when some yo-yo analyst or reporter wrote about what he or she would do if he or she were running Apple. I always thought, "If you think you're so smart and it's so easy, why don't you try to do our job?" Now that I'm on the other side, I won't forget my past.

The world can be divided into two groups: those who make history and those who write about it. Now that I'm in the second group, let me state that I couldn't do a better job than John Sculley. Nor would I want his job for the $2 million to $17 million [depending on options] he makes each year. On the other hand, he couldn't write a column as good as mine, and he wouldn't want to write it for what I make, so we're even.)

Big Blue IBM after Bill Gates squeezed it.

backlash What Susan Faludi and feminists call the "\\" key.

backslash What a Macintosh owner would rather get than use an IBM PC.

backup What wimps do to their hard disks.

> *There are three kinds of people: those who learn to back up before their hard disks crash, those who learn to back up after their hard disks crash, and those who think their hard disks will never crash again.*[1]

---

[1] John Holland.

bad sector MBAs in a company.

> *One MBA can negate the work of six engineers.*

bandwagon A computer that everyone jumps on once there is software for it.

baudy language The abbreviations and symbols used in electronic mail messages. For example: ":-)," "ROTFL," "IMHO," etc. See also *smilie* and "The Unofficial Smilie Dictionary."

> *There are no 9600 baud access lines near your home.*

> *There are no 14400 baud access lines near anyone's home.*

BCIUS Bill Campbell Inherits Used Software—the original code name for Claris.

benchmark The unknowledgeable measuring the unusable for the unbelieving.

beta site A person who is too insecure to wait until a product ships, but too dumb to effectively test it.

> *No matter how many people are beta testing your software, only five will report bugs.*

beta version Software in final testing because the venture capitalists are getting impatient. (Beta is a bastardization of "better" as in, "We're going to ship this software. It's not finished, but it's beta than nothing.")

> *Never buy the "1.0" version of software.*

> *It's okay to buy the "1.0" version of software I endorse.*

Big Blue IBM after Bill Gates squeezed it.

binary Steve Jobs's theory that people are either bozos or insanely great.

BIOS Bozos Insist On Standardization.

bit How much better Windows is than MS-DOS.

bleeding edge People who buy version 1.0 of software.

BMUG Basic Macintosh Unpaid Groupie

> *The higher up a person is sitting in the BMUG meeting hall, the less he or she knows about Macintosh.*

BMW Basic Macintosh Wheels.

board of directors The out of touch, managing the out of control, for the out of sight.

For still more on boards of directors, see "Squeezing The Chairman," at the end of this chapter.

bomb Any software product that sells less than *Lotus Jazz*.

Boolean expression When a spouse says, "True or false: You love your computer more than me."

bozo Someone who sees Windows and thinks it's a Macintosh.

bozosity Standardizing on Windows.

bps Bull Per Second.

buffer The second $5 million of venture capital.

bug A problem with your competitor's product.

> *A problem in your product is an "undocumented feature," or an "unexpected result," but never a "bug."*

bulletin board An electronic communication system created by divorce lawyers to increase their business.

bundle Combining hardware that is too expensive with software that isn't selling.

bus What MS-DOS developers who didn't write Macintosh software missed.

byte What an upgrade takes out of your wallet. See also *gigabyte*, *kilobyte*, and *megabyte*.

More on boards of directors...

Squeezing the Chairman

Reprinted from *MacUser* November 1990

It surprises many people that I take so many potshots at Apple Computer in my column. They misunderstand me. I love Apple, but that doesn't prevent me from criticizing it. I'd like to do all I can to help Apple succeed. This month I'm proposing a really radical idea (I've never been known to lack chutzpah): Elect me to Apple's board of directors.

I'll represent the thousands of shareholders and stakeholders who still cherish the Apple Dream of improving people's creativity and productivity. There may not be enough Apple *shareholders* to elect me to the board, but there are certainly enough Apple *stakeholders* to do it. (A shareholder owns stock. A stakeholder believes in a company's dream.) I think I can do a lot of good, and it would be a blast. This column is my campaign pitch.

The Current Board

The Apple board of directors is presently made up of Peter Crisp, Albert Eisenstat, Mike Markkula, Arthur Rock, John Rollwagen, and John Sculley—as nice, famous, smart, and rich a bunch of guys as you could possibly find. There's only one thing wrong with them: Generally, they really don't use and love computers. Not the way most of us do, anyway.

The problem is that the current board members are too rich and successful. Thus, they have at least one dedicated secretary or administrative aide to do much of their computing. (This is the equivalent of Porsche's board members being chauffeured in a limo.) I suspect that they don't even add paper to their LaserWriters. This assumes, of course, that they haven't already given their Macintoshes to their kids. Don't believe me? Try this test: Send them an AppleLink, and see how long it takes for them to read it and if they respond personally.

The Impact

The impact of not using and loving computers is enormous. First, the directors are easy to fool. I should know—I used to do it. Jean-Louis would prep us on what they wanted to hear, how to gloss over details, and how to get out of trouble. Think about it: What kind of board of directors would approve a 16-pound portable? And then wait for more than a year for a replacement that is barely lighter?

Second, they worry too much about what the financial analysts and pundits are saying. (Mind you, these are the same analysts and pundits who recommended that Apple build an MS-DOS clone in 1983.) Because they listen to these analysts and pundits, they direct Apple employees to do dumb things instead of the right things. How else, for example, could you explain Apple's deep desire to have MS-DOS cards available for Macintosh?

Third, they are out of touch with what computing means for the rest of us. Frankly, no one with a net worth of more than $10 million could possibly know what it's like for the rest of us to own and operate a computer.

My Qualifications

I think I'm qualified. I hope I can convince you too. OK, so I haven't gone into space as Sally Ride has, but I have ridden some shuttles such as the World Trade Center-Bayside and Moscone-Haynes. I also fly coach class with a Portable all the time (I have deformed elbows and slanted eyes to prove it). And speaking of slanted eyes, I represent an oppressed minority—the Japanese-American.

Let me tell you what else I could bring to the current board.

First, I use a Macintosh about four hours a day. Although I'm not technical, very few five-minute, skin-deep, whiz-bang engineering demos fool me. And if I think I'm being deceived, I can ask Andy Hertzfeld what he thinks—not the analysts and pundits (although I might make an exception for Stewart Alsop).

Second, I understand what it's like to be an Apple developer. (Apple developer, *n:* synonym for oxymoron; organization that Claris creates tools for.) I evangelized them, and I was one of them. No one on the current board has a good idea what it's like to be an ant in the jungle when the elephant starts to rock and roll.

Third, I was a rank-and-file Apple employee. While all the honchos are moving employees around the board with the reorg du jour, I know what it's like to be a pawn. I also know what it's like to work at Apple without golden parachutes, golden handcuffs, or golden prophylactics.

Fourth, I am a member of the press. (I am certain of this, because I get a press badge for Macworld Expos without asking.) I know the gruesome details of how the Apple Computer/Regis McKenna PR machine tends to bend, shade, and purify the truth. I also know that everyone knows what it really means when Jean-Louis decides to pursue even better interests.

My Pledge

Read my lips. If elected, this is my pledge: I will represent the computing needs of the rest of us who don't have secretaries, who ride in coach class, and who still care what things cost; I will try to increase EPS (evangelism per share) in addition to earnings per share; and if it's the last thing I do, I will make sure you can call Apple and reach tech support (the phrase "Go back to your dealer" will be banned forever). If it's the second-to-the-last thing I do, I'll ensure that the amount of money we spend making videos is less than the amount we spend on tech support.

It Will Never Happen

One sure thing about my idea is that it will never happen. I would be the last person that Apple would want on its board, because I'd make too much trouble—just as General Motors' board couldn't stand having Ross Perot as a director and finally bought him out. (Actually, I consider not being wanted on Apple's board quite flattering.) On the other hand, anyone else who could represent these points of view and evangelize these objectives could do Apple a world of good. It doesn't have to be me.[2]

[2] About twenty people wrote to tell me that they were writing me in on their Apple proxy. Still, I think I was about six million votes short. I was, however, flattered.

Cray Any computer that weighs more than 100 pounds, requires cooling refrigerant, costs more than a house in Palo Alto, is available in more than one color, and is bundled with two on-site engineers.

cache   Money saved in order to go to Macworld Expo.

CAD   A man who heckles a demonstrator at a user-group meeting. See also *card*.

cancel   What *MacWEEK* will do to your subscription if you don't lie about how many Macintoshes you manage.

> *Right after you start managing the number of Macintoshes you lied about*, MacWEEK will *cancel your subscription*.

card   A demonstrator at a user-group meeting who can handle a CAD. See also *CAD*.

carpal tunnel syndrome A rumor started by pen-based hardware manufacturers.

CDEV Confusing DEVelopment. Software that makes you wonder what's making your Macintosh do strange things.

CD-ROM Crap Displayed Regardless Of Merit.

CGA Color Gone Amok.

chachkas Valueless trinkets handed out at computer shows by companies that can't do good demos.

character An Apple executive.

character set The Apple executive staff.

character string The reporting relationships of Apple executives.

character-based Following the orders of an Apple executive.

chutzpah Pirating software and then complaining about the bugs in it.

The more a person complains about a product, the less the person paid for it.

Claris An experiment to see what happens to a company when its employees are given no emotional, professional, or financial reason to stay.

click The small, exclusive inner circle of computer owners who use Macintoshes.

client Anyone who will pay you to show them how to do what's documented in the manual.

clip art Product development for wimps.

Clipboard To reduce the number of stock options given to board members.

clock speed How fast a company can explain why its software is late.

clone A computer that costs less than $1,000—and takes a $100/hour consultant five hours to set up.

> *You will spend twice the amount of money you saved buying a clone trying to figure out how to use it.*

colon Human SCSI port.

color separation The process that preceeds washing clothes.

columnist A person who can come up with twelve ideas a year and use a spelling checker.

> *A great computer columnist can write three great columns a year.*

> *A lousy computer columnist can write three great columns a year.*

> *Lousy and great computer columnists get paid the same.*

COMDEX 100,000 people trying to find a cab.

> *The first indication that a Macintosh software company is going down the toilet is exhibiting at COMDEX.*

compatible A spouse who lets you connect to E-mail at night. See also *upward compatible*.

> *If you laughed at this definition, you are spending too much time on E-mail services.*

> *If you didn't laugh, you either don't belong to any E-mail services or you aren't married.*

"You will spend twice the amount of money you saved buying a clone trying to figure out how to use it."

compress   Reducing the size of files you should throw away.

CompuServe   The closest thing to dating for nerds.

computer conference   A collection of computer executives in a resort bragging to each other about how smart they are.

For still more on computer conferences, see "Fair Trade Laws," at the end of this chapter.

conditional statement   "If you buy a laptop, you'd better not bring it on our vacation."

conflict of interest   Using a Macintosh but recommending a PC.

co-processor   A spouse who likes to shop.

copy protection   Methods designed to inconvenience legitimate owners and amuse hackers.

Never, ever buy copy-protected software.

The only way to effectively stop software piracy is to create software not worth stealing.

Many companies have effectively stopped software piracy.

copyright   The directive that Bill Gates issued to his MS-DOS programmers when they first saw a Macintosh.

CP/M   Computing Prior to Microsoft.

crash   When your competitor's product dies.

When your product dies, it's called an "unexpected termination," but never a "crash."

"The only way to effectively stop software piracy is to create software not worth stealing."

Cray Any computer that weighs more than 100 pounds, requires cooling refrigerant, costs more than a house in Palo Alto, is available in more than one color, and is bundled with two on-site engineers.

creeping elegance A Lexus 400 SC almost out of gas.

cropping Layoffs at Aldus.

cybernetics Evangelism on steroids.

More on computer conferences...

Fair Trade Laws

Reprinted from *MacUser* April 1990

Copyright © 1990, Ziff Communications Company

The goal of this column is help you get the most out of the April 1990 Macworld Expo in San Francisco (or any other Macintosh show). It represents the knowledge I've gained by attending or exhibiting at every Macworld Expo except one. (I missed the August, 1986 Expo because it conflicted with my wedding, and I couldn't convince the show promoter, Mitch Hall, or my wife-to-be to change dates.)

Industry-Day Power Plays

Industry day is the day before Macworld Expo opens to the public. In theory it is for Very Important Pessimists to coolly and calmly walk the floor. In reality, it gives software vendors one more day to figure out why their new version is crashing and to train new employees: "Trixie and Biff, this is a mouse. The ball goes on the bottom and the button on the top."

Industry day is a farce because almost anyone can get a pass. All you have to do is appeal to the greed, competitiveness, and paranoia of vendors. Call a vendor and say, "I'm from Boeing (or any other Fortune 1,000 company). I'm responsible for the selection of Macintosh software and would like to discuss standardizing on your product. Is industry day a good day for you?"

It helps if you really are from Boeing or a Fortune 1,000 company. If you aren't, saying that you're a consultant to one of these companies is good enough. Ask the vendor to send you a badge (vendors get an allotment of them), and after it comes, call and cancel the meeting. If you feel guilty, tell the vendor that you'll come to its booth. Whether you actually go is up to you. Most vendors won't remember the conversation anyway.

On the Floor

I recommend the minesweeper approach to seeing the show: going up and down every aisle to see every vendor's booth. The only booths that you should skip are the ones with skits, barbershop quartets, and models—unless, of course, you enjoy having your intelligence insulted. If you're pressed for time, here's a quick analysis of the booths not to miss.

Apple. Tiny companies with very innovative products often exhibit in the Apple booth. Usually these companies are not anywhere else in the show, so the Apple booth is the only place to see them. On the other hand, the unavoidable yet-another-HyperCard-stacks and Popular Science-induced videos could ruin your whole day.

Claris. The Claris booth staff is typically friendly and informative because product managers, tech support engineers, and trainers staff it. This is especially true at the

San Francisco show because it's close to Claris' head-quarters in Santa Clara. Also, they have nice carrying bags.

Microsoft. The Microsoft booth is interesting to visit if only to see how Microsoft is trying to crush its competitors—for example, vaporous pre-announcements to negate a competitor's shipping product. The Microsoft booth always provides a great lesson in guerrilla marketing.

Silicon Beach, CE Software, and Qualitas Trading. Silicon Beach people are extraordinarily friendly, and their Aloha shirts make me homesick for Hawaii. CE Software people love to do demos. If they really like you, they might even send you some incredible Iowa pork chops. Qualitas is the cool Japanese company with the cool Japanese clip-art and cool calligraphy software.

How to Get Free Stuff

At some point you are going to have to justify your trip to your company or spouse. The best way is to get free stuff. Free stuff can range from Wingz bags that break in 10 minutes [*Two years and counting on mine.—Ed.*] to product samples. I'll assume that you want to concentrate on the latter.

As with getting industry-day passes, you simply need to appeal to the greed, competitiveness, and paranoia of vendors to get free samples. The key is to believe in your heart that you are doing the vendor a favor. A list of the ploys that always worked on me follow.

1. I'm a reviewer for *MacUser*. I'd like a copy of your software to review. Microsoft and Claris have already sent me copies of their products. [*Umm… We—and our lawyers—strongly discourage this*

practice; besides, it doesn't even work for us all *the time.—Ed.*]

2. I'm the president (or librarian or newsletter editor) of the Macintosh user group in (city). I'd like a copy of your software to review. Microsoft and Claris have already sent me copies of their product.

3. I'm responsible for the selection of software for my company. I'd like a copy of your software to review. Microsoft and Claris have already sent me copies of their product.

4. I'm a Macintosh consultant. I'm sick of recommending x (where x = a competitive product). I'd like a copy of your software to review. Microsoft and Claris have already sent me copies of their product.

Desktop Partying

During Macworld Expo there are wonderful parties throughout San Francisco. Their sole purpose is to impress competitors and to reduce corporate income taxes (i.e., waste money). The best places to try are the hotels that are close to the Moscone Convention Center, such as the Parker Meridien and Marriott.

It is your inalienable right to attend and enjoy as many parties as possible. After all, you've paid for them, and most vendors dread the prospect of an empty party.

There are three kinds of parties: the ones that start immediately after the show, the ones that start at 7:30 P.M., and the ones that start at 10:00 P.M. The first kind always has great buffets. The last kind always has great desserts and dancing. I recommend that you go to these.

The second kind, the 7:30 bashes, are not worth attending. They are usually stuffy, sit-down affairs that are filled with people who really don't want to be there. Some go out of corporate obligation. Some go out of boredom. Some go because their spouse made them.

Be There or Be Square

There you have it—a guide to optimizing your Macworld Expo experience. I hope to see you on industry day carrying lots of free software in your Claris bag and looking well-fed. I'll probably be at the Microsoft booth taking notes.[1]

---

[1] Within months of the appearance of this column the people who run Macworld Expo canceled industry days.

demo Someone who doesn't know anything, showing software to people who don't believe anything, accomplishing nothing.

dating The process prior to merging.

> For still more on dating, see "The Macintosh Guide to Dating and Marriage," at the end of this chapter.

DAL Dreck Access Language.

debugging The process that begins one week prior to Macworld Expo.

dedicated Working ninety hours a week and loving it.

default The initial setting of a program to its most illogical state.

defragment Laying people off and moving to a smaller building.

demo Someone who doesn't know anything, showing software to people who don't believe anything, accomplishing nothing.

<blockquote>*The larger the audience is, the more likely and spectacular will be the crashes in the demo.*</blockquote>

<blockquote>*The most effective way to find crashing bugs is to do a demo at BMUG. See also* BMUG.</blockquote>

desk accessory Doing in 200K what can be done in 1400K. See also *application*.

desktop Proof that a noun can become an adjective.

desktop publishing A secretary with PageMaker.

diagnostic program A program to tell you what you already know: your file is fried.

dialog What you would like to have with the designers of Microsoft Word.

digital Anything hard to read in direct sunlight.

dimmed What happened to Claris's prospects when Apple brought it back.

dim sum A telecommunications error-detection technique that doesn't work.

DINC Double Income, No Clones.

disk cache Money saved to buy a bigger, faster hard disk.

Display PostScript John Warnock's 911 Carrera/4. See also *Encapsulated PostScript* and *PostScript*.

<blockquote>*"The larger the audience is, the more likely and spectacular will be the crashes in the demo."*</blockquote>

DIP switch Going from MS-DOS to UNIX.

documentation Stuff no one reads that comes with software.

DOS Domination Of Society. See also *MS-DOS*.

DOS Boot A movie about how Bill Gates forced his Macintosh application programmers to work on DOS 5.0.

double density Someone who has worked in both marketing and sales. See also *high density* and *single density*.

downtime The time spent interacting with other humans.

DPI Dollar Per Icon The amount Microsoft offered Apple to license the Macintosh user interface. (This amount, deemed piddly by Apple, caused the Apple/HP/Microsoft lawsuit.)

drag When your company standardizes on IBM PCs.

drive, external Money.

drive, internal Pride.

dumb quotes An explanation for shipping delays.

> *Use smart quotes and apostrophes.*
>
> *Except for inches and feet.*

dumping Japanese companies selling products for what American companies claim it costs to make the products.

The Macintosh Guide to Dating and Marriage

(Reprinted from *The Macintosh Way*)

"Behind every successful man there stands an amazed woman."

Anonymous

In case you read this book and you don't run a company, here's a real-life application of the Macintosh Way. This chapter explains the Macintosh Way of dating and marriage.[1]

Beth and I did the *MacWEEK* ad because it was fun and because we admire *MacWEEK* for its fearlessness. We wanted the headline to read, "Only two things really excite my husband, and he gets one of them only once a week," but *MacWEEK* wimped out. Maybe they aren't so fearless after all.

"Only two things really excite my husband."

High-Tech Dating (For Men)

There are six good women for every good man in high technology, so I will concentrate on helping more men break into the "good" range. Frankly, it will do men more good because men need more help. This is the right way to date (for men).

1. **Position yourself as a tool.** High-tech women are not masochists—they have careers that are as interesting and important as yours. To be attractive in this kind of market, you have to be a tool, not a problem. Do something useful like checking her

[1] The people who read drafts of [The Macintosh Way] were split almost exactly 50/50 on this chapter. Half said that I should take it out because it has little to do with running a business. Half said it was the best chapter of the book. I left it in—after all, this is my book.

hard disk for viruses (but not on the first date) or debugging her 100,000-line assembly language program.

2. **Treat your date like she is the only platform in the world.** Put this on your floppy disk and write-protect it because this is the key to successful dating. The Joe Isuzu dating paradigm—Italian suits, leased teutonic wagons, cellular phones, and IPOs—do not equal kindness and attention as user-friendly features. Inter-operability is not a desired feature in dating.

Exercise

Rent a Ford Escort. Ask the most desirable woman you know for a date.[2] Try to impress her.

3. **Maintain an open architecture.** An open system is as important for dating as it is for personal computers. Possessiveness too early is a big mistake, so don't close the system until the proper, mutually satisfying configuration is reached. It's not like software—don't announce, then ship, then test. Instead, go alpha, then beta, then golden. You may be living with this release a lot longer than with your software.

4. **Form strategic alliances.** It's puzzling that men who spend all day forming, preannouncing, and announcing strategic alliances cannot apply the same techniques to their social lives. Strategic alliances with friends, roommates, and family can make or break you in high-tech dating.

Friends and roommates are likely to shape a woman's initial opinion of you. They probably

[2] Dating is when two people go someplace where there are no computers, talk about anything except computers, and do analog stuff afterward.

know all her old boyfriends and are comparing you from the first moment you meet.

Also, when you get serious, it's not with a person but a family. It's easier to sell The Macintosh Office without a fileserver than date successfully without parental approval.

5. **Never ignore your installed base.** No matter how good things are going, never ignore your installed base (i.e., your old girlfriends). They can provide advice, add mystery and challenge if someone is taking you for granted, and introduce you to more women.

6. **Here are some final tips for Macintosh men.** Put them in ROM[3] and solder in the chip:

- Always believe it's your privilege and honor to be with your date.

- Never be late.

- Aspire to be best friends.

- Don't be afraid to show weakness.

- Never criticize your date in public.

- Never compare your date unfavorably to anyone except her mother.

[3] ROM stands for Read-Only Memory. That's the place in a computer that doesn't go away when you shut off the power. It's also the place where computer companies put their worst idiosyncrasies.

High-Tech Dating (For Women)

Well, honey, let's face the sad news: the odds are against you. There are very few men worth competing for (and many good women you are competing with) so you have to do what's necessary to date high-tech men.

1. **Make yourself more physically attractive.** When it comes to women, men, all men, especially

high-tech men, can see better than they can think. Sad commentary but true. High-tech men are body by Volkswagen, brains by Cray, heart by Frigidaire, personality by Metamucil. And all men are SCSIs.[4]

2. **Hang around high-tech joints.** If you want to meet high-tech men, you've got to hang around high-tech joints like Fry's Electronics[5] or COMDEX.[6] I never said it would be easy or pleasant. Try to get to Fry's around dusk so you can see the nerds watching the sun set over the Santa Cruz mountains.

3. **Take the first step.** Most high-tech men are as sophisticated as the UNIX interface when it comes to taking the first step, so you are going to have to take the initiative. Unplug the AppleTalk cable from the Laser Writer and then hang around until they show up trying to figure out what went wrong. Shutting down the Apple Share fileserver would work too. Do something. Anything.

Exercise

Which opening line do you think would work best with a Macintosh man?

A. Would you zap my parameter RAM?

B. Haven't I seen your Navigator face file before?

C. What's your file type and creator, handsome?

D. Want to see my PICT files sometime?

E. My disk is fragmented. Do you know where I can get SUM?

[4] SCSI stands for Small Computer System Interface. It is the name of the type of port or orifice on Macintoshes. Thus, "all men are SCSIs" is an adaptation of a frequently heard phrase when single women get together.

[5] Fry's Electronics is the ultimate nerd store in Silicon Valley. At Fry's you can buy Jolt, DRAMS, chips (both the kind you plug in and get fat on), and CDs all in one place.

[6] Comdex is a computer show that is held in Atlanta and Las Vegas each year. It is supposed to be for retailers to see upcoming new products. In reality, it's just a bunch of employees from hard disk manufacturers who go to each other's booths to look at the latest in platters.

4. **Get it up front.** Don't put up with a vesting period. A good rule of thumb for engagement rings is one carat of diamond per computer. My wife says that a Laser Writer counts as a computer because it has a 68000[7] in it.

Somehow a woman married me, so this advice must work. Being married, however, definitely affects your career path. When I first thought of starting a company, I asked my wife Beth if she would still love me if I left Apple (and its salary, options, and profit sharing).[8] Her reply was, "Of course I'll still love you. I'll also miss you."

I've found that what made you fascinating to date can make you "shallow" and "narrow-minded" after you're married. When I was dating my wife, she thought it was the coolest thing that I was a big deal in the Macintosh community. Now, she'd like to take a sword to my—I mean our—poor Macintosh.

Beth and I have been married for over three years now, and I believe that getting and staying married rounds out and balances your life. She worked at Apple in the Seattle office and then in Cupertino, so she's been infected by Macintosh too. Recently she quit Apple to do what she really wants—design clothes—and we went from DINC to SINC.

Working at Home—Beth 1, Guy 0

Working at home is productive because you're not interrupted by phone calls, meetings, and other distractions. I do my best work at home alone in the solitude of Macintosh bliss.

Unfortunately, spouses believe that time at home should

[7] A 68000 is the name of the Motorola chip that is the brains of a Macintosh. 68000s have broken up more marriages than affairs, drugs, and fast cars combined.

[8] Profit sharing is what's left after paying for the senior executive bonuses, the leased Mercedes, the fresh orange juice, the first class flights, and the Bösendorfer grands.

be shared. The key to being able to work at home is to convince your spouse that by working extra hard your company will achieve success sooner and you can vacation more and retire earlier. If you figure out the right way to do this, I'd appreciate hearing from you.

Exercise

A woman started a company. She worked long hours and traveled a lot. After a year, the company was successful, and the woman came home earlier, didn't bring work home, and was generally attentive. She and her husband live in Portola Valley, they have two beautiful kids, and they vacation at the Mauna Lani four weeks each summer.

The best title for this passage is:

A. The World According to Kleiner-Perkins

B. Yeah, Right.

C. Mauna Lani Customer Profile

D. The Long Term Effects of Reality Distortion

E. If You Lose Your Dream You Die

There are three additional techniques that you can use to slide past your spouse. First, pay a little attention to your spouse before you start working. A little bit of attention— a kiss, a hug—when you enter your home can add a few hours to Mac time. I try to wait at least 60 seconds before I get on my Macintosh.

Secondly, try to incorporate some of your spouse's interests in your conversation. Because my wife is interested in fashion design I try to talk about the implications of Display PostScript[9] on her field. This doesn't work quite right.

Thirdly, convince your spouse that you are creating art, not working or playing on your Macintosh. My wife let me work on this book (and therefore my Macintosh) for many hours because I told her that "I'm writing, not working on my Macintosh"—à la Ernest Hemingway, J.D. Salinger, or Colette. This works all right for a while.

CompuServe—Beth 2, Guy 0

CompuServe and the four other electronic bulletin boards that I belong to drive my wife nuts. She can't understand how I can spend so much time E-mailing total strangers. She especially can't deal with how amusing I find Navigator[10] face files.[11]

The 2400-baud line for CompuServe requires a message unit call where we live. One month we had a $200 message unit bill. Mind you, this was not the CompuServe bill (I have a free account), this was the phone bill. I'm no dummy; now I use a toll-free number so she can't see how often I sign on.

Exercise

Send me an EasyPlex on CompuServe. My account is 76703,3031. Ask me if Beth wants me off the computer.

This leads me to explain the right way to get on and stay on CompuServe and other electronic bulletin boards:

[9] Display PostScript is a graphics language developed by Adobe Systems. Apple is so upset about the royalties it pays Adobe for PostScript in its printers that it refuses to adopt Display PostScript for its displays.

[10] Navigator is a program that makes access to CompuServe easier. It should have reduced people's connect time to CompuServe, but it has had the exact opposite effect. Now people connect more often and longer because it is easier. I don't think CompuServe planned it this way, but it's better to be rich than smart.

[11] Face files are pictures of the sender and recipient of messages on CompuServe so that everyone has an idea of what the people look like. Clever people even make the lips of the faces move.

- Get a separate data line[12] so you don't fight for the phone.
- Turn off the modem speaker so she can't hear you connect.
- Have the phone bill go to the office.
- Have the CompuServe bill go to the office.
- Use software that autoconnects at preset times.

Business Travel—Beth 3, Guy 0

My wife hates it when I go away on business. If you've ever seen me speak at a user group, you know I arrive in the afternoon and fly out the same evening. I bet you thought it was because I had some important business meeting to attend.

At first, my wife used to come with me on business trips so that we could travel together. That didn't last long because she didn't want to be around me when I'm with other Macintosh nerds. It seems that our conversations don't cover the full gamut of music, literature, and art.

I even tried to convince her that an August vacation in Boston would be fun. There are a lot of historical things to see in Boston, like the World Trade Center,[13] and we wouldn't have to bring any warm clothes. Now I bring her back a mouse pad from every city I visit. She is somewhat less appreciative than one might hope.

So Who's Keeping Score?

We are not going to win this battle. I've come to the conclusion that the right thing to do is pay more attention to our spouses than our Macintoshes. That is, until we get our laptop Macintoshes...

[12] This way she won't pick up the phone and have the modem carrier tone screaming in her ear and her friends won't tell her that the phone was busy for hours.

[13] The World Trade Center is where the Boston Macworld Expo is held every August—about half of the Boston Macworld Expo, anyway. The only thing worse than its location is its air conditioning.

Eddy award winner A product you haven't heard of, revered by editors who don't use it, in categories you can't figure out.

earnings per share The meaning of life for Apple executives.

Eddy award winner A product you haven't heard of, revered by editors who don't use it, in categories you can't figure out.

> *Products that win awards from magazines don't necessarily become commercial successes.*

> *But they do generate a lot of advertising.*

editor A person who claims that he has no budget for a larger advance, no time to read your draft, and no authority to promise marketing.

Behind every successful author stands an amazed editor.

electronic mail A method for receiving messages you cannot understand, from people you don't know, concerning things you don't care about.

> *The larger your monthly E-mail charges, the less likely you'll stay married.*

> *Each year a person is married adds one hour of connect time per month.*

For still more on electronic mail, see "E-mail Etiquette," at the end of this chapter.

em dash The size of the space between Lauren Hutton's teeth.

Emess DOS The Jewish operating system.[1]

emulation Using software that enables your computer to run applications you don't care about, slower than you can stand.

Encapsulated PostScript Apple's efforts to reduce Adobe's royalty payments. See also *PostScript* and *Display PostScript*.

enhanced keyboard Any keyboard not sold with a PC Jr or Apple IIc.

ergonomics The study of the problems Macintosh users encounter when they try to use an IBM PC.

Ethernet Software that makes you think your network is faster.

EtherTalk Promises of a quick update.

evangelism Convincing people to buy things they don't need but cannot do without.

---

[1] "Emess" is Yiddish for truth—a special kind of truth, as indicated by this story. A Jewish man went into a store to buy a computer. A Jewish salesperson showed him a Macintosh and a clone running Windows. After listening to the salesperson explain the advantages and disadvantages of both for an hour, he asked, "Tell me the emess. Which would you buy?" The salesperson replied, "The emess. Macintosh."

*It takes three years for a company to evange-
lize a great collection of software for a new
computer.*

*It takes another year for the market to realize
it.*

*By the time the market realizes it, another
computer is introduced.*

evangelist Someone who sells dreams—as opposed to
someone who dreams of sales.

*You don't have to recruit evangelists for your
cause. They will come to you.*

export What Japan does.

extended memory Anything over 640K.

More on electronic mail...

E-mail Etiquette

Reprinted from *MacUser* November 1991

Copyright © 1991, Ziff Communications Company

This is a thread of public E-mail messages recently posted
on CompuServe. It concerns the quality of Jean-Louis
Gassée's column in *MacWEEK* and mine here. It inspired
me to write about E-mail etiquette.

```
From: Barry House

To: Tim Fredenburg

Tim,

I'm with you. Gassee appears to be trying
to be a "devil's advocate" who offers a
```

*"You don't have
to recruit
evangelists for
your cause. They
will come to
you."*

wildly different viewpoint. Unfortunately, he often succeeds only in presenting a half-formed idea with a conclusion that is seldom supported by the bulk of his text.

Instead of Mac celebrities like Gassee in MacWEEK and Kawasaki in MacUser, I'd rather read someone who has something genuine to say and writes well in saying it.

- Barry

From: Guy Kawasaki

To: Barry House

Barry:

Are you saying that (a) I have nothing to say or (b) that I don't write well or both? I doubt that the MacUser people will see this comment here in the MacWEEK area. You should contact Jim Bradbury (72511,41) directly to complain about me.

Guy

From: Barry House

To: Guy Kawasaki

Guy:

Actually, I'm saying both. On the other hand, you ARE Guy Kawasaki, so mediocre copy with your byline is more marketable than mediocre copy with my byline. I have the same problem with Monsieur Gassee; I can't think of a column he's written for MacWEEK—or you've written for MacUser—

that would have been accepted if it had been submitted by me or some other unknown freelancer.

- Barry

Here is the "Guy Kawasaki Guide to E-mail Etiquette."

In Your Face

1. Ask yourself, "Would I say this to the person's face?" before you post a public message. I don't know Barry personally, and I feel that meeting him would be right above being Iraq's representative to the United Nations, but I suspect that he's an average Joe like any of us. Electronic mail, however, turns average Joes and Janes into swaggering John Wayne-Steven Seagal-Chuck Norris-Charles Bronson-mutant-ninja-electronic assassins.

Ask yourself this question, and keep editing until the answer is yes. Then your message may accomplish something. Otherwise, your message will probably be ignored, because most people know that E-mail turns normal folks into raging savages. In my case, I don't ignore these messages: I take great joy in them and go so far as to reprint them in a column so that 375,000 people can read them too.

2. Give your E-mail recipients cues about what you really mean. In person-to-person communication, you provide many cues such as your facial expression, voice tone and volume, and body stance. Imagine the difference between reading a message that says You're a lousy writer and a face-to-face conversation in which a person says the same thing and then smiles. It's possible to communicate these cues on E-mail through the use of E-mail symbols and abbreviations.

Here are a few from Ken Schoenberg and the rest of the gang from America Online and from *The Unofficial Smilie Dictionary*, sent to me by someone from Internet:

:)	=	Smile
;)	=	Wink
:(	=	Frown
:-(O)	=	Yelling
$-)	=	Just won the lottery
=:-)	=	Hosehead
:-'	=	Spitting out tobacco
:D	=	Laughing
:*	=	Kiss
: X	=	Lips are sealed
[:-)	=	Wearing a Walkman
:P	=	Sticking out tongue
[]	=	Hug
LOL	=	Laughing Out Loud
OTF	=	On The Floor (Laughing)
ROTFL	=	Rolling On The Floor Laughing
\V/_	=	Vulcan greeting

When you get good at using these, you can be rude without being rude. For example, `If you think my writing stinks, you should smell your breath sometime. :)`

3. When you send mail, think of the easiest way for your recipient to respond. For example, if you're on AppleLink and your recipient is on AppleLink, send your message through AppleLink. Some people send mail via Internet (a worldwide network that links E-mail systems) to an AppleLink recipient even though they have an AppleLink account, because Internet is free. The problem is that when the recipient responds, he has to type an address like Joe_Blow@tuck.edu@internet#.

If you want an answer, make it easy for the recipient—not cheaper for you. I often incorrectly address Internet responses, and by the time I get the message back, I've thrown away the original message. Also, I'm not all that sure how Internet works; I think that Clifford Stoll runs Internet from his house and forwards all the messages in his spare time.

4. Never send a file when a message will do. When you send a file, you're saying to the recipient, "You have lots of time to waste. I want you to download the file. Remember that you downloaded it. Remember where you downloaded it. Remember its name. Decompress it with a utility I assume you have. Open it with an application I assume you have. If you don't have the decompression utility or application, write back to me to ask me to send it another way."

After a guy has downloaded and opened a file, he has the privilege of reading a three-paragraph message in a font he doesn't own. Of course, you could have copied and pasted this file into a message with three clicks of a mouse. Is there any legitimate reason to send a file? Yes: when many people are *working* with the file. For example, a file should be sent between a writer and an editor or between a desktop publisher and a Lino parlor.

5. If you have to send a file (although I can't see why you have to, other than the reason I just mentioned), put your

E-mail address into the file. Many people send files that don't contain their E-mail address, so the recipient has to go back online and search for the sender's address. This is the '90s equivalent of mailing a letter without a return address on the (dumb) assumption that the envelope stays with the letter.

6. Keep it short. E-mail should save time, not waste it. Rule of Thumb No. 1: No message should be longer than 100 words. Rule of Thumb No. 2: A response should be a fifth as long as the inquiry (for example, 100-word inquiry, 20-word response).

Most messages are drawn out and meandering messes: "I bought the first Apple II in my city while I was an undergraduate at Boise State concentrating on East Asian studies until I became a COBOL programmer at American Airlines where I worked on an IBM 360 while I attended night school in a nursing degree program until I bought a Macintosh 128K (gee, the *1984* commercial was neat-o) with a green carrying case and a free copy of MacWrite and MacPaint (gee, isn't Bill Atkinson a genius)..."

E-mail is GIGO: Get In and Get Out. Ask your question, get your answer. E-mail flattens out corporate and sociological hierarchies. You can write to John Sculley, John Akers, or the Dalai Lama without going through assistants. They respond. It's as simple as that. Nobody cares who you are. Everybody cares about wasting time.

7. Ignore stylistic and grammatical considerations. Using E-mail saves time because careful editing and proofing is not necessary or appropriate. E-mail is supposed to be fast, tit-for-tat communication. You ask. I answer. You ask. I answer. You're not supposed to watch the sun set, listen to the surf pound the sun-bleached sand, and sip San Miguel beer as Paco dives for abalone while you craft your E-mail.

Between Me and You

8. Never use receipts and carbon copies. Receipts are messages the E-mail system generates to inform the sender that the recipient has read the mail. You know what carbon copies are. Receipts are insulting. You are saying to the recipient: "You're a lazy schlub who never reads his E-mail. I receipted this message so that I know you read it. Now you have no excuse not to answer, because I know you received the message."

Carbon copies are stupid. For example, I often get carbon copies of messages sent to John Sculley complaining about Apple. People who send these think that John is going to see that I'm carbon-copied and be scared fecesless that I'll write about the matter in *MacUser*. Or that by bringing the matter to my attention, I'll be so overwhelmed with concern that I'll intercede and call John to help resolve the problem.

Dream on: John couldn't care less that I've been carbon-copied—assuming that he even notices it—assuming that he reads the message. Dream on: When I get carbon-copied, I usually throw the message away. (E-mail etiquette stipulates that if it ain't addressed to you, you ain't got to do anything about it). I have enough problems being a wife without getting involved in other people's problems.

A Declaration

This column has been cathartic. It is also a declaration: Ninty-five percent of the people who send me electronic mail will probably read this, so from this point on, if you send me a file, you will not get a response. If you receive files from people, send them a photocopy of this column.

If this is too much trouble, contact me, and *I'll* send you a file of this column to send to them. ;)

And let me know if you'd like a copy of *The Unofficial Smilie Dictionary*, and I'll send it to you—also as a file.[1]

---

[1] I got dozens of requests for *The Unofficial Smilie Dictionary*. That's why it's in the S chapter of this book. Please observe these rules if you send me E-mail.

flame   The process of showing how petty you are by leaving inflammatory E-mail messages.

fatal attraction The Apple/IBM alliance. See also *fatal error*.

fatal error The Apple/IBM alliance. See also *fatal attraction*.

> *Europe will be unified before the Apple/IBM alliance produces a product.*

fax E-mail for wimps. See also *E-mail*.

FCIUS French Company Intended to Upset Sculléy—the code name for the company Jean-Louis Gassée started after he "left" Apple.

female connector Electronic mail for a nerd.

FIFO First In, First Obsolete.

Finder A Macintosh application that could do everything except find files.

FINO First In, Never Out.[1]

flame The process of showing how petty you are by leaving inflammatory E-mail messages.

flat-file database Any database that is fast, easy to use, and sells in large volumes.

FLOPS Companies that a venture capital firm invests in that don't go public. (Usually preceded by "mega-" or "terra-.")

footprint The amount of space an IBM PC wastes on your desk.

fractal Apple's organization chart.

fragmentation The space on your hard disk between files you should have deleted.

frozen The condition of software on the day before Macworld Expo.

> *Of all the software you ever buy, be sure to send in the registration card for software you bought at a Macworld Expo.*

FUD Flaccid, Uninspired, and Dubious—a term coined to describe IBM's personal computer efforts.

fuzzy A program's degree of System 7 compatibility.

"Of all the software you ever buy, be sure to send in the registration card for software you bought at a Macworld Expo."

---

1 Thanks to Alan Touchberry.

greek To place nonsensical text prior to placing confusing text.

The prettier the document, the less the content.

gigabyte The cost of one billion upgrades. See also *byte*, *kilobyte*, and *megabyte*.

GIGO Goys In, Goys Out.

glare The look on MS-DOS users' faces the first time they see you select a printer with the Chooser.

greek To place nonsensical text prior to placing confusing text.

>*The prettier the document, the less the content.*

GUI Gates Used Intimidation. Also, Good Until Investigated (MS-DOS bigot version).

Sleeping with the Enemy

Reprinted from *MacUser* September 1991

Copyright © 1991, Ziff Communications Company

Let me be subtle: Microsoft is the enemy. It seeks to dominate and control personal computing. Microsoft would like to ship every piece of software you use—even the operating system—and squeeze every other software company out of the market. Microsoft tolerates hardware companies like Apple and IBM, seeing them as OEM suppliers. If there weren't such a low profit margin in hardware, Microsoft would be building computers too.

Don't get me wrong: Microsoft is a tremendous company and a great example of excellence in American business. I admire what Bill Gates and his company have accomplished. But I don't have to like it. And I don't have to stop trying to head off Microsoft at the pass before it achieves a monopolistic position. So here's my plan to save us all from being controlled by Microsoft.

Catalyze Microsoft Arrogance

First, let's help Microsoft become so arrogant that it no longer feels the need to introduce new products or enhance existing ones. Arrogance leads to the downfall of companies. Lotus springs to mind. In the late '80s, Lotus believed that its 1-2-3 spreadsheet was such a powerful standard that people would buy it "just because."

The problem is that Microsoft still believes that it must compete for business. It refuses to rest on its laurels (except with Microsoft File, which has set such a high standard for Macintosh databases that it hasn't required revision). We must change this attitude and make Microsoft believe that we will buy its products "just because." Every time you speak to Microsoft employees, tell them how wonderful all Microsoft products are, how Microsoft sets the standard in every category, and how you "would buy a Microsoft product just because of the Microsoft label." Try to do this with a straight face—especially those of you who own Microsoft Works, PowerPoint, and Microsoft Mail. (Hey, I never said that implementing my plan would be pleasant.)

Also, you could tell MBA students to go to work for Microsoft after graduation. (Sending over people who were laid off from Oracle would have the same effect.) The more MBAs at Microsoft, the better, because most MBAs are convinced they should be running companies after two years of reading case studies. As a rule of thumb, one MBA can neutralize the impact of five good engineers.

Free Claris

On one hand we must ensure that Microsoft gets arrogant and begins to decay. On the other hand, we must ensure that other companies take up the slack—especially Claris. Claris was created for two reasons: to establish a kick-ass competitor to Microsoft and to end the competition between Apple and its developers. Both reasons still make sense. Perhaps they make even more sense today, because of Microsoft's megalomaniacal tendencies. Unfortunately, Apple Kuwaited Claris, bringing it back into the Apple galaxy as an internal division. Why? Apple says it realized the importance of application software and wanted to control its destiny in this area.

I think Apple executives got sick of hearing Claris executives brag about their plans to go public and then do Windows software. I can't blame the Apple executives for getting upset at this, but Kuwaiting Claris was the worst thing they could do.

Why? Because as an Apple division, Claris won't be a kick-ass software company. It will be subject to Apple's quarterly-earnings paranoia. Now Claris is going to be more worried about helping the mother hardware company than about delivering great software. Claris will be a dumping site for all the projects Apple doesn't want to manage—projects that no real software company would consider. I'm sure Gates thanked his lucky stars for the day Apple Kuwaited Claris.

(Speaking of Gates and Kuwait, let me interrupt to tell you a story that illustrates how powerful Microsoft has become. At the Apple Worldwide Developer's Conference in May, 1991, Apple invited Bill Gates to help introduce System 7. Unbelievable! Tell me that George Bush went to the grand opening of Saddam Hussein's new chemical weapons plant. Or that Iraq's ambassador had a goodwill tour of Northrup's stealth-bomber facility.)

My plan calls for the liberation of Claris. It should be an independent software company with the sole mission of becoming the world's greatest Macintosh developer—the Microsoft, if you will, of Macintosh. Claris should have a software company's perspective: do what's right for *software* customers—not only for Apple customers who've bought the parent company's hardware.

Should Claris do Windows software? At first glance, the answer is of course not. Apple could retain 51-percent ownership and so every plan to do non-Apple-platform software. On closer inspection, the answer is not so simple. Imagine Claris providing the leading Windows applications. Then Apple (with its majority ownership) could threaten Microsoft the way Microsoft threatens Apple: "We don't like what you're doing, Bill. If you don't do things our way, we may not revise WindowsWrite II, and we may ship the NeXT version of Resolve sooner."

Every time you speak to an Apple employee, express concern for what's going to happen to Claris and request that Claris be an independent software company. It would help if you're from a large company (such as Boeing, General Dynamics, EDS, Kodak, or ARCO) because Apple tends to listen to companies that are potential purchasers of thousands of Macs. Apple will also listen to those who can say they're from universities such as Carnegie-Mellon, the University of Chicago, or Stanford, because Apple is afraid of the inroads NeXT is making in higher education.

Distract Gates

The Japanese have a saying: "Where the head goes, the body will follow." The head of Microsoft is Bill Gates. He is smart, tough, and ruthless—frankly, he'd be an ideal CEO of Apple, and this may be the subject of a column someday. Another part of my plan is to distract Gates— and the rest of Microsoft's upper management—so that they run the company less efficiently.

Here are a few ways to do this. First, those of you who are in graduate schools of business should invite Gates to speak at your school. While there, he may meet a business school student, fall in love, and get married. This isn't that farfetched—just ask Steve Jobs. You know that anyone strong enough to marry Gates is going to demand a high level of attention from him. This will reduce his ability to make business trips, work late, and work at home.

Second, those of you who can write compilers should contact Gates and tell him that you've created a revolutionary object-oriented BASIC and that Claris is trying to acquire it. I don't know why, but Gates has this thing about BASIC. It would really bother him if Apple—er, Claris—were going to sell one.

Third, those of you who always wanted to start a company should create one now and announce products in any category that Microsoft doesn't yet occupy. This will force Microsoft to preannounce a competitive product in order to grab that market. Any of you who already have products that compete with Microsoft's should announce new versions so that Microsoft has to preannounce a new version in order to kill yours.

Fourth, those of you who decide to take my advice in the previous paragraph should call the Federal Trade Commission as soon as Microsoft makes its preemptive strike. Tell the FTC that Microsoft is competing unfairly with you. The FTC's telephone number is (202) 326-2222. On second thought, you shouldn't do this. If I had to bet on Microsoft or the FTC, I'd bet on Microsoft.

Create and Consider the Alternatives

This brings me to the last part of my plan for overcoming Microsoft: All kidding (and the FTC) aside, the only thing that can really defeat Microsoft is superior products. This requires two things: superior products and people having open minds about considering alternatives to Microsoft products.

The first necessitates that developers get off their self-pitying, fat derrières and make great products. It also requires that venture capitalists take risks. (Otherwise, they should just invest their funds in Microsoft stock and then go play golf and sip martinis at the Sundeck every day.) The second requires that people buy the best product for their needs—Microsoft or not.

Here are some alternatives to consider: CE Software's QuickMail instead of Microsoft Mail. WordPerfect or Claris' MacWrite Pro instead of Microsoft Word. Aldus Persuasion instead of PowerPoint. Add to this list two products you probably haven't heard of. The first is an integrated product (code-named "Terminator" which should give you an idea of its purpose) being created by Robert Hearn and Scott Holdaway of Claris. Terminator will blow Microsoft Works into the weeds. And you can quote me. (It may be shipping by the time you read this column.) The second is an ingenious product that combines spreadsheet and database functionality. The Objective of creating this product is to take on Excel. However, I'm on the board of directors of the company that's creating it, meaning that writing about it is a conflict of interest, so I'll stop right here.

Don't kid yourself—Microsoft wants it all: from operating systems to application software. Only your ingenuity and open-mindedness can save the day. Are you a (wo)man or a Microsoft mouse?

Helocar $25 million spent convincing Yuppies to use a Macintosh to design cars with helicopter blades.

hacker Genius untapped.

handle The layer of fat around the belly of management.

hard copy Anything that can incriminate you in a lawsuit.

hard disk A device that enables you to keep files you don't need.

> *Buy twice as much hard disk space as you think you'll need...*

> *...and delete half of the files you think you should keep.*

> *The optimal size for a hard disk (in bytes) is three times a person's annual salary. (Subtract 1,000,000 for Apple executives.)*

hardware Any product with less than 50% margin.

head seek time Whenever earnings per share slip.

Helocar $25 million spent convincing Yuppies to use a Macintosh to design cars with helicopter blades.

hertz A unit of measure used to determine how good a programmer is, as compared to Andy Hertzfeld.

heuristic If a person doesn't "get" Macintosh in the first thirty seconds, he never will.

hex Using Windows on a 286 machine.

hexadecimal Using a network of 286 machines running Windows.

HFS Hidden Folders Suck.

high density Having less than six engineers to counteract each MBA.

highlight The video portion of an Apple press conference.

hindsight We should have put more RAM in the first Macintosh.

For even more on hindsight, see "Just Undo It," at the end of this chapter.

HyperCard Apple System software (1988–1990). Apple Application software (1990–1991). Claris neglected software (1991–present).

HyperTalk Apple executives after drinking two espressos.

More on hindsights...

Just Undo It

Reprinted from *MacUser* July 1992

Copyright © 1992, Ziff Communications Company

This is the last column I'll be writing for *MacUser.* I'm giving it up, because the editors of the magazine felt that my investment and involvement with After Hours Software and Salient were inappropriate. Specifically, *MacUser* requested that I cease and desist using my picture in ads for After Hours Software.

I tried to go along with this separation of Guy the columnist and Guy the huckster, but after a couple of months, I concluded that it was a farce. I informed the editors that I was going to allow After Hours Software to use my picture, and the editors and I decided that it would be best for me to ride off into the sunset.

I see the editors' point and their perspective, and life goes on. Maybe it's the best thing for both of us—for me, anyway, because it is going to force me to go beyond Macintosh and the computer industry in my writing.

Beyond Macintosh

When you make a big decision like this, your mind goes through many gyrations: Should I give up my column to sell a few more copies of TouchBASE and DateBook? Will people forget who I am? Will this be a mistake I'll regret?

This got me to thinking about other decisions I've made and the hindsights I've accumulated in 38 years of existence on this planet. If I could do my life over again—if I could just undo it—what would I do differently? What truths have I discovered? What insights can I pass on to others?

This got me to thinking about decisions other people have made in their lives. What would they have done differently? What truths have they discovered? What insights would they like to pass on to others? What can we garner from the knowledge of our senior citizens (that is, anyone older than 38)?

This got me to thinking that the hindsights of people would be a great topic for a book. All kinds of people: rich, poor, powerful, powerless, famous, unknown. Teachers. Waiters. Clerks. Mechanics. Criminals. Billionaires. Ministers. What oral history and lessons could they leave so that people wouldn't make the same mistakes and could optimize their own lives?

So I decided to start another book. Its working title is *Hindsights* (however, the marketing mavens at my publisher may change that). I am going to interview people around the United States to document their hindsights about life: education, family, money, love, and work—whatever they want to talk about and pass on.

All modesty aside, I've written two books about how to change the world. Now I'd like to write one about how to understand it.

My role model is the writer Studs Terkel. He concentrates on interviewing blue-collar workers and how they feel about their lives. I want to interview a broader cross section of people and find out how they feel about their past. To give you an idea of what I'd like to do, here are some of my hindsights about high school and college.

High School

I was a diligent Oriental in high school. I studied hard. I never cheated. I took college-level classes and earned college credits, so that I could graduate early and work the rest of my life. I studied Latin, because it helped me more easily expand my vocabulary, in that many English words are derived from Latin.

I played football. I loved football. (All you Gloria Steinem wannabes should skip this paragraph.) Football is macho. I was a middle linebacker, arguably one of the most macho positions in a macho game. Very few feelings are equal to a good "stick" when you blitz the quarterback or when a wide receiver comes across the middle. (Getting System 7 to work on the first try is one of them.)

French, Music, and Tennis

Hindsight #1. Machismo aside, if I could do high school all over again, I would **learn a foreign language,** because today it's very difficult to have a conversation in Latin other than at the Vatican. And despite all my efforts to evangelize evangelism, the Pope has yet to call for my advice. You never know: If I had learned French, maybe I would still be at ACIUS. If I had learned French, maybe I would never have started ACIUS.

Hindsight #2. I would **learn to play a musical instrument.** My only connection to music today is that I was named after Guy Lombardo. (Trust me: It's better than being named after Guy's brother, Carmen.) If I'd learned to play a musical instrument when I was in high school, I could be playing it now and enjoying it for a long time. Instead, I have to buy CDs and be at the whim of the Tower Records buyers.

Hindsight #3. I would **play a noncontact sport** such as tennis. That is, I would play a sport that you can play as you cross over into the golden years beyond 38. Today it's difficult to get 22 guys together in a stadium to play football—probably as difficult as having a conversation in Latin. On the other hand, all the guys who wore cute white outfits and played tennis in high school can still play tennis. Meanwhile all the macho football players are sitting around watching television, drinking beer, and worrying about arthritis in their knees.

College

I was a diligent Oriental in college too. I rushed through in three and a half years. I never attended any of the overseas campus programs, because I didn't see how doing so would help me make money and it would delay my graduation. I hardly ever traveled except to return home for vacations and to meet my mother and father in Las Vegas for hands-on training in statistics and probability. I never even went to a Grateful Dead concert.

Hindsight #4. If I could do college over again, I would **stretch my college education, travel as much as *my parents* could afford, and live off them as long as possible.** I would take whole semesters off to travel after attending the overseas campuses in Italy, France, Germany, Japan, and any other country. This would extend college to at least six years.

This means I would delay for as long as possible the inevitable entry into the workplace and the lifetime of servitude to bozos who knew less and worked less but made more money than I did but were still unhappy.

People have to work the rest of their life—what's the rush? I still wouldn't, however, go to a Grateful Dead concert.

Macintosh Hindsights

This is a Macintosh magazine, so I have to include some Mac hindsights. Here are two:

Hindsight #5. **You can't give software developers too much RAM.** We should have shipped the first Macintosh with 256K of RAM. It would have made software development easier and accelerated the availability of software by 9 to 12 months. We mistakenly thought that everyone could program like Andy Hertzfeld.

Hindsight #6. **Creating a "closed" system was one of the smartest things we did.** By closed, I mean that the first Mac didn't have slots and didn't have Apple II or IBM PC compatibility. This meant a shortage of software for a while, but it forced developers to create pure from-the-ground-up Macintosh software. Thank God for Steve's insistence on purity.

Hindsight #7. **A columnist has an obligation to his readership.** In the past several months, my mood has become arrogant and detached. (Some people may dispute *become*.) Thankfully, a reader made me aware of this by telling me that he was disappointed that my column about technical support communicated the feeling of "don't bother me with your technical-support problems."

Then I was crushed when my mother told me that my column about programming was "wrong and we don't like it," because I told people to send their software directly to my church instead of to me. My father was also on the phone, and he said that I had a noblesse oblige to the readers to show more class than that. (Where he learned French, I don't know; I never did.)

They were, of course, right. I should not have written those columns that way. On the other hand, I have no regrets about my columns about Singapore; Microsoft; the National Rifle Association; John Sculley; and, especially, being a wife.

A Little Help from My Friends

I hope this column made you reflect on your life and come up with hindsights and insights. Perhaps you would like to share some of your hindsights. Also, I need referrals to people to interview. If you know extraordinary people whose hindsights would be valuable, please tell me about them.

Extraordinary does not mean rich, famous, or powerful. It means people who have contributed to society and who can contribute more by telling their story. They don't need to have any connection to Macintosh and computers. In fact, I prefer that they didn't. Here's how to get in touch with me: P.O. Box 471090, San Francisco, CA 94147; 415-921-2478; 415-921-2479 (fax); 76703,3031 (CompuServe), Kawasaki2 (AppleLink), or MacWay (America Online).

You take care of yourself. And as Arnold said at the police station, "I'll be back." While I'm gone, just remember a few things:

- Do the right thing, the right way.

- No job is worth a marriage.

- Enjoy your family and friends before they are gone.

- Buy any piece of software I endorse.[1]

---

[1] Dozens of people suggested very interesting folks to interview. My favorites, however, were the 25-year-old Wall Street stockbrokers who suggested themselves.

interface That which justifies Apple's margins.

I/O Ignorance/Obsolescence.

IBM Take your pick: International Bowel Movement, I'd Buy a Mac, Intimidated By Microsoft, or Incredibly Boring Machine.

icon 1,024 pixels doing the work of five letters.

illegal character An Apple executive without a green card.

IMHO In My Hardass Opinion.

INIT I No It's Trouble.

> *Half of the INITs running in your Macintosh are unnecessary...*

> *...and the other half of the INITs conflict with each other.*

insertion point An entry-level marketing position.

Installer A utility that copies software with too many features onto your hard disk.

> *"Install 1," no matter what you do with your Macintosh, is the disk you will use most often.[1]*

> *Software that needs an installer is hard to use.*

Intel The Greek god of trade tariffs.

integrated software Software that David Duke won't use.

interface That which justifies Apple's margins.

italics The style of printing obtained when paper goes in the printer crooked.

invisible characters Apple fellows.

IPO Initial Premature Offering. Transferring financial risk from venture capitalists to the public.

ISDN I Swear Debate's Necessary.

"Software that needs an installer is hard to use."

1 Beginning with System 7.1, "Install 1" is simply called "Installer."

Jolt Steroids for programmers.

job Any activity that provides money to buy cars.

> For still more about jobs, see "Get A Job," at the end of this chapter.

Jolt Steroids for programmers.

> *The more Jolt programmers drink, the shorter the software development cycle…*
>
> *…the more Jolt programmers drink, the more spectacular the bugs…*
>
> *…most programmers drink too much Jolt.*

Jungle Fever A movie by Spike Lee that explains the Apple/IBM alliance.

> *If the Apple/IBM alliance was so important, why wasn't John Akers at the press announcement?*

Still more on jungle fever...

Silicon Fever

Can't believe that Apple and IBM have an alliance? Here's how the idea for the alliance started. You finish it. Cut out the puppets, fold over the tabs, and place them on your fingers.

The Players

John Sculley (Chairman, Apple Computer, Inc.)

John Akers (CEO, IBM)

Bill Gates (CEO, Microsoft)

with a special appearance by Spike Lee

Act I

John Sculley: Microsoft is going to kill Macintosh with Windows.

Curtain.

Act II

John Akers: Microsoft is going to kill OS/2 with Windows.

Curtain.

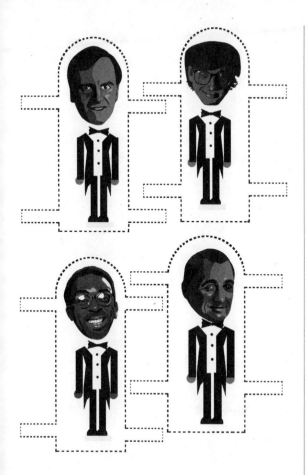

Act III

Bill Gates: I'm going to kill Macintosh and OS/2 with Windows.

Curtain.

Act IV

John Sculley: I'll call John Akers. Maybe we can do something together to survive.

Curtain.

Act V

John Akers: I'll call John Sculley. Maybe we can do something together to survive.

Curtain.

Act VI

Bill Gates: What could Apple and IBM do? Ally with each other?

Curtain.

Act VII

Spike Lee: Haven't you seen *Jungle Fever*?

Derisive laughter.

Curtain.

---

justification, engineering "Marketing changed the specs."

justification, marketing "Engineering added more features."

More on jobs...

Get a Job

Reprinted from *MacUser* June 1992

Copyright © 1992, Ziff Communications Company

This column will explain, in 1,600 words, how to get a job in the Macintosh industry. I'm writing it because I get nearly 100 letters or E-mail messages each month from young people asking for career advice. You won't find this kind of advice in any book or get it from any job counselor, because the Macintosh industry isn't "any" industry.

Start Your Product Development Early. Think of yourself as a product. Think of your education as product development. Don't wait to start worrying about your job search until immediately before you ship—that is, graduate. The time to start is the summer between your freshman and sophomore years of college.

Every summer, while your buddies are getting tanned and drunk in Ft. Lauderdale or Palm Springs, you should intern at any company that will take you. Work for free if you have to. Shine John Warnock's shoes. Empty Paul Brainerd's trash can. Clean the Windows at Microsoft.

At the end of three years, you'll be able to document your experience in the Macintosh community. Along the way, you should be able to pick up a good recommendation or two. Maybe one of the companies will even hire you. Getting a job is like dehydration: If you're thirsty, it's too late.

Don't Start Out Working for Apple. Many graduates think that working for Apple is the coolest thing. It can be, but you can also seriously and permanently damage yourself. This is because Apple's idea of new-employee training is to throw people into the water and see who can swim. You won't get managed. You won't get trained. You won't get mentored.

If you can "swim," this can work to your (temporary) advantage. You may, for example, start as a college hire and end up managing a group within three months. You'll think that this is the fast track, that you've found a company that appreciates your management potential (at age 22), and that working for Apple is like being paid to go to Disneyland.

More on jobs . . .   **87**

The problem is that the real world isn't like Disneyland. You'll start *believing* that you know what you're doing, and you'll turn into an Apple puke. And, until you get laid off, you'll have delusions of grandeur that will pervert your mind. Someday, when you discover the real world or the real world discovers you, you'll be in deep trouble.

Instead, go to work for a company, such as Proctor & Gamble (or even IBM), that has a training program. Unless you work for an organization that has tradition and discipline, you won't fully develop your skills. And you'll never fully appreciate how great it is to work for an Apple unless you've worked somewhere else.

The First Job Doesn't Matter. And the second one doesn't either. Too much emphasis is placed on finding the "perfect" first job, because you think you're going to work your butt off for a few years, cash in your stock, and retire when you're 30.

Instead, don't be picky and proud: Just get a job—even a lousy one at a good company. Then work hard, and transfer to a better job. Face it: The difference between most graduates and a can of Alpo is that the can of Alpo has content. The crucial step is *getting in,* not *advancing.* Burrell Smith, the wizard who designed the original digital boards for Macintosh and the LaserWriter, was working in Apple's service department when Jef Raskin recruited him to work on Macintosh.

If you want to try the theory of "just get in," go to work for a Macintosh temporary agency such as MacPeople (2490 Channing Way, Suite 516, Berkeley, CA 94704; [415] 548-1147). Sooner or later, you'll get an assignment at a Macintosh company. Do a good job, and the company may offer you a job. Do well. Get promoted. And remember me when you're rich and famous.

More on jobs . . .

Take the Shotgun Approach. The goal of a job search is to get a job, not necessarily to get a job *through established and official procedures.* Everyone knows that you're supposed to apply through the personnel or human-resources departments. But there are many people competing with you: Apple Computer, for example, gets as many as 10,000 résumés a month. (This column might reduce that number.)

If you color only within the lines, you'll get what life hands you. I recommend coloring anywhere there's paper. This means contacting nonpersonnel people such as technical-support engineers, salespeople, and executives. The more shots you take, the more shots you'll make.

Don't be afraid that a company is so coordinated that all your applications will be forwarded to one person who'll say, "This jerk has applied all over the company. He won't get past me."

Don't Take the Shotgun Approach. There is one place where you shouldn't use the shotgun approach: the description of your qualifications. Many peoples' résumés claim "expertise in PageMaker, Photoshop, QuarkXPress, 4th Dimension, SQL, MacDraw, Microsoft Word, and Lightspeed C." What *doesn't* the person know?

The corporate reaction to this kind of shopping list of qualifications is, "Yeah, right. Another overinflated know-it-all who's God's gift to computers." Expertise—true expertise—in any one of these products is good enough. Saying that you're an expert in all of them is a case of "more is less."

Such people as Ole Kvern, Robin Williams, and David Blatner have spent years learning FreeHand, PageMaker, and QuarkXPress. Do yourself a favor, and watch *The*

More on jobs . . .

Karate Kid before you write your résumé. Then go learn one or two programs extremely well. You'll know you're good when you feel like writing a book about using the product.

In your job application, mention only the products you know very well. Underpromise and overdeliver on your expertise. Bring up your breadth of knowledge in the interview—not in your cover letter and résumé.

Don't Drop Names. Many applicants drop people's names to try to get in the door: "John Sculley loved my HyperCard stack," "Steve Bobker said I'm the best PageMaker designer he's ever met," or "Jean-Louis Gassée really liked my database designs."

Dropping names seldom works, for two reasons. First, who cares what Sculley, Bobker, Gassée (or Kawasaki) thinks? At this point, they (we) are all living off our reputations.

Second, if a company checked with Sculley, Bobker, Gassée (or Kawasaki), it'd find out that they might not remember meeting the person. This is because being a Macintosh figurehead means meeting thousands of people every year, and no one, not Sculley, Bobker, Gassée (or Kawasaki) can remember meeting everyone—no matter how incredible they are.

Sculley, Bobker, Gassée (or Kawasaki) are required to be polite and attentive, however. A person who interprets this behavior as "He really likes me. He'll really go to bat for me" is being deluded. I don't know what Sculley, Bobker, or Gassée do when someone calls them for a reference, but I often tell the company that I have no idea who the person is.

Drop the Graphics, Fonts, and Photographs. Keep your cover letters and résumés short and simple. Most of the letters and résumés I get are one page too long—that is, they're two pages. No one—not Steve Jobs, Lee Iacocca, Akio Morita, or George Bush—especially a recent graduate, needs more than one page for a résumé.

Also, drop all the special effects: the scanned image of your face; the outlined, shadowed, boldfaced fonts; and the Martha Stewart-inspired fleur-de-lis border around the edges. Just because PageMaker can do it doesn't mean it's appropriate for a job search.

Use a sans serif font for the headings and a serif font for the body, and be done with it. Some companies scan in the resumes they receive. You may think you're impressing a recruitment person, but you're actually confounding a scanner. One page. Two fonts. No graphics. *Capisce?*

Go with the Flow. These actions lead up to one goal, getting an interview. You have only one thing to accomplish in it: show that you want to change the world in a manner that is consistent with the company's vision. Here are the keys to an effective interview.

1. **Prepare.** Read everything you can about the company. This is a no-brainer, and every book written about job searches says it. Most graduates must have no brains or cannot read, because hardly anyone does this. You have to know the company's vision before you can show how you can fit into it.

2. **Shut up.** Let the interviewer do 80 percent of the talking. You want the interviewer to think you are quiet and thoughtful, not loud and brash. I never heard of anyone saying too little in an interview.

More on jobs . . .

3. **Listen.** Many interviewers will tell you what they want to hear. For example, "We value team players at MegaloSoft." The right response: "It would be an honor to join the MegaloSoft team. I think I could really learn a lot from others and make a solid contribution too." The wrong response: "My professors have always told me that I am genius programmer. They say that my code is art. When do you think I can head my own engineering team?"

4. **Follow through.** Also a no-brainer. Within a day of your interview, write a thank-you letter to everyone who interviewed you. Again, hardly anyone does this.

Last Resort

If all else fails, go to work for a DOS or Windows company. I hear they have lower standards. And if you make a lot of money, give some to your parents for taking care of you all these years. Then go change the world.

Macworld A Macintosh magazine for people who like pretty pictures and unintelligible bar graphs.

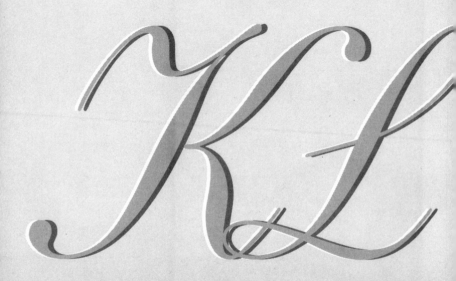

kerning To shorten the time span between upgrades in order to improve the appearance of a company's commitment to its customers.

kilobyte The cost of one thousand upgrades. See also *byte*, *megabyte*, and *gigabyte*.

kluge See *Windows*.

More on kluge/ Windows.

The Top Ten Reasons to Switch to Windows

10. So you can spend $2000 upgrading your $1000 clone to run as slow as a $1500 Macintosh.

9. So you can help debug the first versions of new software.

8. So you can find out how a Macintosh owner felt in 1986.

7. So you can see for yourself how little industry analysts know.

6. So you can give your Macintosh to your six-year-old kid to do desktop publishing.

5. So you can feel comfortable wearing a w-i-d-e, yellow, paisley tie.

4. Because you believe MS-DOS is a solid foundation for new system software.

3. Because you heard that Steve Bobker is starting a magazine called *WindowsUser*.

2. So you can understand why Andy Hertzfeld, Steve Capps, Bill Atkinson, *et al* may never be equaled.

1. So you can help pay for the federalization of Bill Gates's 959.

---

landscape   What the Japanese would do if they weren't dumping chips and cars. See also *dumping*.

laptop   Any computer weighing less than six pounds and costing more than $3000.

LaserWriter   A device that jams when you're in a hurry.

lawsuit   The process of turning pigs into sausages.[1]

LCD   Long, Costly Delays—the result of the American tariff on Japanese screens.

---
[1] With due credit to Ambrose Bierce.

LED Lunacy-Emitting Dealer.

letter quality When a company's tech support is so bad that you feel compelled to send a letter to its president.

> *A fax works better than a phone call which works better than a letter.*

license agreement The gibberish on the envelope that contains the software that you're about to pirate.

LIFO Last In, First Obsolete.

load The amount software entrepreneurs expect to make.

localization Translating software for markets that pirate it.

LocalTalk Ethernet without hormones.

log off To end a relationship.

log on To begin a relationship.

logic Whatever Regis McKenna, Incorporated says it is.

look and feel What Bill Gates would start suing over if anyone ever copied Microsoft's software.

> *Always look before you feel.*

luggable Whatever Jean-Louis Gassée says it is.

MBA Madness, Bozosity, and Arrogance.

MacBinary Someone who has a Macintosh at home and at the office.

Macintosh Technology that Xerox invented, Apple borrowed, and IBM is trying to exploit.

> *"A fax works better than a phone call which works better than a letter."*

During the first three months, you love your Macintosh. During the second three months, you hate it. During the third three months, you understand it.

Using a Macintosh is like sex: when it's good, it's very good. When it's bad, it's still good.

For still more on Macintosh and Mac Mastery, see "Masters of the Macintosh," at the end of this chapter.

Macintosh Weigh, The   The amount of weight the Portable lost to become the PowerBook.

MacUser   An advertising medium for columnists with conflicts of interest.

Macworld   A Macintosh magazine for people who like pretty pictures and unintelligible bar graphs.

Macworld *is for Yuppies;* MacUser *is for geeks.*

The number of mice or stars a magazine awards to a product bears no relation to its suitability for you.

Each mouse or star is good for 2,000 additional copies of the product sold per month.

Macworld Expo   30,000 people trying to get an invitation to Ingram/Micro D's party.

The big, dumb, and rich companies are in the World Trade Center.

The small, smart, and poor companies are in the Bayside Exposition Center.

The software you bought just before going to Macworld Expo will cost 25% less at the show.

The software you bought just before going to Macworld Expo will have a new version at the show.

mainframe Any computer with more than one blinking light on the outside.

Never trust a computer you can't lift.

Never lift a computer you can't trust.

marketing The closest thing to telecommunications for a Yuppie.

mastering The mass reproduction of bugs.

MAUG Maligned Apple User Group.

Media Lab (MIT) Proof that you can find funding for anything if you try hard enough.

megabyte The cost of one million upgrades. See also *byte*, *kilobyte*, and *gigabyte*.

memory management The ability of computer executives to forget what they promised customers, employees, and shareholders.

menu-driven A Macintosh owner with bulimia nervosa.

merge The process of creating clones.

Microsoft Bill Gates' biceps.

Over the course of owning any Microsoft product, you will spend twice as much on upgrades as you did for the product.

MIDI Mixing Is Delightfully Intuitive.

minicomputer A computer that is heavier than ten pounds and unusable by mortals.

MIPS Macintosh Is Pretty Slow.

"Over the course of owning any Microsoft product, you will spend twice as much on upgrades as you did for the product."

MIS   Meshugge Information System.[1]

More on MIS...

The Three Biggest Lies Told to Fortune 500 MIS Departments by Macintosh Evangelists

3. Macintosh can run MS-DOS software.

2. Macintosh can connect to an IBM mainframe.

1. Macintosh requires less training and support than a PC.

---

motherboard   The nickname of the board in the Macintosh that was the hardest to design.

Motorola   Apple's brains.

mouse   Doug Englebart's favorite animal.[2]

MPW   Macintosh Programming Witchcraft.

MS-DOS   Microsoft Seeks Domination Of Society.

> *The interest from the interest from the interest from the interest from the interest of Bill Gate's net worth exceeds your annual salary.*
>
> *Bill Gates is no happier than you or me.*

MTBF   The length of a warranty plus one day.[3]

MultiFinder   Software that enables more than one application to crash at the same time.

[1] "Meshugge" is Hebrew for crazy, nuts, ridiculous, or absurd.

[2] Doug Englebart is the inventor of the mouse. He is arguably the first person to place great emphasis on designing user interfaces so that mere mortals could use computers.

[3] Some people think MTBF stands for Mean Time Between Failures, but their computer never broke.

multimedia   The unnecessary in search of the
undoable.

> *The more a speaker uses multimedia, the less
> he or she has to say.*[4]

> *The greatest barrier to multimedia had not
> been addressed: the projector.*

multitasking, cooperative   Crashing one application at a time.

multitasking, preemptive   Crashing more than one
application at a time.

*"The greatest
barrier to
multimedia had
not been
addressed: the
projector."*

More on Mac masters...

Masters of the Macintosh

Reprinted from *MacUser* February 1992

Copyright © 1992, Ziff Communications Company

I don't believe in the tooth fairy, I don't believe that the
check is in the mail, and I don't believe in the Apple-IBM
alliance. Still, even if this alliance never yields a product,
it will have one immediate, powerful effect: it will legiti-
mize Macintosh.

Now when Apple employees, dealer salespeople, and
Macintosh evangelists face the objection that the Macintosh is just a "cute, graphics toy computer," they can
retort, "If it's GUI enough for IBM, it's GUI enough for
you." This is worth a lot.

[4] Thanks to John
Holland.

Let's face it—this means that a lot of novices, beginners, and Great Un-Macintoshed Masses are going to be using Macintoshes very soon. This column is for them: it explains how to master a Macintosh. I don't expect you to need it—simply photocopy it for your friends.

Definitions

There are three kinds of Macintosh users; I call them hackers, obsessives, and masters.

Hackers buy or pirate every product, install every utility, download every shareware product, and reformat their hard disks once a day. They go to product demonstrations and try to stump the speaker with inane questions such as, "How many rules of Codd and Date's Relational Model does your database adhere to?" Hackers describe System 7 this way: "It's terrific. I only crash twice a day." Hackers don't achieve mastery because using a Macintosh becomes an end rather than a means.

Obsessives are hackers with less brains. If they were athletes, they would buy $300 designer workout suits but never sweat. They read every book, they listen to all the audio training tapes, and they read the ReadMeFirst! documents. Initially, their Macintosh experience is so wonderful that they think they've mastered Macintosh in the first week. Then they hit a wall, get frustrated, and give up—blaming Macintosh, not themselves.

Masters understand that using a Macintosh is a means to an end. They understand that mastering a Macintosh is like climbing a series of hills and that each hill gets you further up the power curve. Using a Macintosh to them is a lifetime journey. Their path is analogous to martial arts experts who don't "arrive" but constantly improve and raise themselves to a higher state.

Diagnosis

Before we get started let's determine which kind of Macintosh user—master, hacker, or obsessive—you are. Sharpen your pen-based input device, and take this short quiz:

1. Which statement best describes you?

- I can't get any work done. I'm still looking for the perfect application or the perfect next version so I can finally get started. When it arrives, I'll start.

- Even though I've spent more than $5,000 on books, training, and tapes, I still can't use a Macintosh very well. It's a stupid computer after all...

- I like my Macintosh OK. It's not perfect, but it helps me get the job done. I have to go right now to make some bank deposits.

2. When a software developer announces a new version of an existing product, what is your reaction?

- Call the developer and demand that you become a beta site or you'll switch to a competitor's product.

- Call Personal Training Systems and MacAcademy to find out if there are tapes or classes for it.

- Smile to yourself for a second before you go to the bank to make a deposit.

3. When you heard about the Apple/IBM alliance, what was your reaction?

- Called John Sculley to offer your services as a consultant to help design the next computer architecture, because you have ten years of C programming experience.

- Went to Nordstrom to buy a new three-piece suit and a yellow tie so you can be properly dressed to use this new computer.

- Laughed uncontrollably before going to the bank to make a deposit.

If the first choice for each question describes you, then you are a hacker. If the second choice describes you, you are an obsessive. If the third choice describes you, you're either a master or a liar.

The Road Less Traveled

Here is how to travel along the road to Macintosh mastery:

1. **Set your expectations correctly.** It takes about fifteen minutes to set up a Macintosh, but it takes about two years to master it. When you first start using a Macintosh, you swallow huge gobs of gains in productivity, creativity, and enjoyment. The size of the gains, however, gets smaller and smaller as you achieve mastery. Using a Macintosh is like skiing: it takes only about a day to get started but years to get good.

2. **Go with the flow.** The process of mastery is not only long but is also cyclic. There are times of great satisfaction and great frustration. When you are frustrated, keep working on it until you bust through to the next level. Expect setbacks along the road to Macintosh nirvana. Sometimes you'll even think that you're regressing, and that you're getting worse at using a Macintosh.

3. **Be bold: experiment and play with your Macintosh.** Don't worry about making mistakes or hurting your Macintosh. It really takes a lot of

effort to damage your Macintosh, applications, or files. If you're curious about what will happen if you try something, go ahead and try it. You may lose some work, but even that will be instructive. If you don't take chances, you won't know, so try things such as turning off your Macintosh while it's printing. You'll find that a Macintosh is almost bulletproof.

4. **But don't be stupid.** Although it is difficult to damage your Macintosh, that's no reason to go looking for trouble. If you suspect that you may be doing something dangerous, back up your files or ask other people's opinion first. I would draw the line at doing anything to your hardware, so be very careful when you "open the hood." You can harm your Macintosh or get a charge (electrical, that is) out of your Macintosh.

5. **Read voraciously.** I swear there are more people writing about Macintosh than using it. There are hundreds of books about Macintosh and Macintosh software. Some of them are get-mediocre-quick and merely repeat what the manuals say. Many, however, provide insights that authors gained over years of Macintosh mastery.

6. **Don't blame your tools.** A craftsman doesn't blame his tools, so don't blame your Macintosh. A sushi chef doesn't blame his knives. A painter doesn't blame his brushes. A writer doesn't blame Microsoft Word. The software may be slow, buggy, or missing features, but the blame is ultimately yours. Blaming your tools is wimpy: fundamentally, you either do a job or you don't.

7. **Join a user group.** User groups are Apple's unpaid evangelists, providing technical and emotional support to Macintosh users. They can help smooth out the road during your Macintosh journey. Almost every question you may have about a Macintosh has probably been answered before, and going to a user group is a good way to meet people with the answers. There are over 1,000 user groups located around the world. To find one in your area, call Apple's information line at (800) 538-9696, ext. 500. If you join a user group and I'm there doing a demo, don't ask me any inane hacker questions.

8. **Join an electronic-mail service.** There are more than five million Macintosh users out there. At least a thousand of them know more than you do, and these people live (literally *live*) on electronic mail services such as America Online and CompuServe. If you join a service, you can post questions and people will answer them. The answers aren't always right, but what do you expect without charge? To get information about America Online, call (800) 827-6364. To get information about CompuServe, call (800) 848-8199.

9. **Don't buy the first version of software.** Have you ever noticed that most new software ships in early January or early August? That's right around a Macworld Expo. Did you think this was a coincidence? It's not. Software companies rush to ship software at these times, which lowers quality control. (Corollary: If a company was going to ship a new product at Macworld and doesn't, it really had a lot of bugs.) Trust me: let other people test new products; keep working, and get the .01 version.

10. **Don't upgrade too fast either.** Have you ever noticed that most new versions ship in early January and August too? You can see where I'm headed. Upgrading is like getting married: I've never heard of anyone getting married too late, but I've heard of many people getting married too early. Trust me: Let other people test new versions; keep working, and wait for the bug fix. I'm still using, for example, System 6.0.5.

11. **Save your shekels.** From the moment you get your Macintosh, start saving money for your next Macintosh (or maybe another personal computer). Personal computers change rapidly, so you'll probably want to buy a new computer or upgrade your current one in 12 to 18 months. Accept this fact, and start saving for your next purchase. Sometimes achieving mastery means having to fork over more dough.

There you have it: how to master using a Macintosh. The road is long—never ending may be a better description—but worth it. What other "thing" can bring you so much enjoyment, productivity, and frustration? Using a Macintosh is just about the most fun you can legally have with a machine.

nanosecond   Apple's attention span.

nanosecond Apple's attention span.

nerd, nerdette Someone who considers CompuServe a dating service.

> *The odds of finding Mr. or Ms. Right on an E-mail service are less than the odds of Microsoft discontinuing Windows.*

network Finding unemployed people you know.

NeXT   A computer that provides the promise of today, on your desk tomorrow.[1]

For still more about the NeXT, see "Deja Vu," at the end of this chapter.

non-disclosure agreement   An agreement between two parties not to tell each other's secret to anyone except Mac the Knife, Cringely, and Spencer the Kat.

> *Ninety percent of what non-disclosure agreements cover is already publicly known…*
>
> *…and the other ten percent isn't interesting.*

NTSC   Not That Stupid Computer.

Num lock key   Giving MBAs options that vest over four years.

More on NeXT...

Deja Vu

Reprinted from *NeXTWorld* magazine

"NeXT Computers. This is Tracy."

"Hi. I'm a Macintosh developer, and I'd like to get information about writing software for NeXT."

"Okay, one moment please."

"Hello. This is Susan."

"Can I get information about writing software for NeXT. I'm currently a Macintosh developer."

1 Thanks to John Holland.

"The first step is for you to fill out an application to become a certified developer for us, and I'd be happy to send you an application…"

Elapsed time: 45 seconds.

Already, I knew I was in trouble. NeXTWorld had asked me to write a column about NeXT's efforts to evangelize third-party software and hardware developers, and I was set to write a scathing report about NeXT's arrogant, unresponsive, and yellow-tie evangelists (NeXT calls them "advocates") who wouldn't be able to evangelize Christianity if they'd seen the resurrection.

This pre-conception was a misconception. I found, much to my disappointment, that NeXT evangelism is among the best in the personal computer and workstation computer industry. In fact, much of NeXT's evangelism is reminiscent of the heyday of Macintosh evangelism in 1984 and 1985. I'm a pragmatist: If you can't criticize someone, you might as well claim that they're as good as you were.

NeXT evangelism starts at the top—or near the top. The person in charge of developer programs at NeXT is a vice president who reports to Steve himself. This is a big deal because it shows that developers are as important to NeXT as R&D, sales, and finance. (This isn't reminiscent for me. The highest I could get at Apple was a director—and then only if Jim Manzi, Ed Esber, and Bill Gates approved.)

In evangelism (and sex), position and size aren't the key. What counts is performance, and NeXT's evangelists are exemplary. Here's why. First, the evangelists really believe the crap that they are saying. I had a role-playing session where I was the Macintosh developer and two evangelists tried to convince me to do NeXT software. I said, "You're only selling 3,000 units a month. Macintoshes are selling 100,000 per month. How can I make money doing a NeXT product?"

They said: "✔NeXT is the direction for the future of computing. ✔We represent a growing marketplace when other manufacturers are flat. ✔You can be on the leading edge of computing which will help you with your products on the other platforms. ✔Though we have smaller run rates, you can penetrate more of the market because there is less noise."

It doesn't matter if these reasons are true. Good developers want to write software for a computer before it's rational anyway, and all that they want is to hear is reinforcement of their unfounded decision. Thus, the most important thing is that evangelists believe their own crap, and the NeXT evangelists certainly do. (To tell you the truth, Macintosh evangelism succeeded because we were too dumb and naive to know that it shouldn't.)

Second, the evangelists know how to use reality distortion. The evangelists told me that the NeXT has a 50% market share of the "professional workstation" market. You've got to love this malarkey: define a new market by subtracting the (Sun) workstations sold for engineering and scientific uses, so that you can claim an impressive market share. (The Japanese have a saying: "If you can't make the numerator rarger, make the denominator smarrer.") Why if NeXT defined a market for black professional workstations, they could claim 100% market share.

Third, the evangelists have the right attitude: "Ask forgiveness, not permission." That is, they will do special things for developers such as sliding them loaner equipment, giving them free passes to developer training, and paying the travel expenses for them to visit NeXT. These kinds of actions, no matter how inconsequential they may seem as you read this column, foster loyalty to a company.

Talk is cheap so I asked the evangelists for references. In real time, the NeXT evangelists rattled off three developers and their phone numbers. (The fact that they had the phone numbers memorized is a significant fact that should not be overlooked.) These references checked out though I wonder what would have happened if I called other developers.

Fourth, the evangelists know how to play their cards. It's common for evangelists to get NeXT's engineers and managers to meet with developers to discuss the developer's products, to hear their concerns, and to offer technical advice. I asked, hypothetically, if Steve (the ace in the deck) would come to my NeXT product announcement. The answer was an immediate "Yes." To a developer, this is the equivalent of the Pope agreeing to baptize your child—before it is born.

Finally, NeXT has created effective developer programs and tools including a developer training course that's run twice a month in California, once a month in Pittsburgh, and once a month in Europe; a ten-volume documentation guide to writing NeXT software; and online bulletin board support. It's not only informative, it's also reassuring to developers that such programs and tools exist.

If NeXT's evangelism is so good, why is there so little software? I've been in this position before, so let me explain. First, it always takes two to three years to get software. Always. Nothing can change this. Second, from the time a computer has great software, it takes another year for the industry to recognize this. Let's face it: most of the computer press is dumb.

Third, NeXT evangelism wasn't always this good. NeXT initially had the misguided belief that it was a privilege and honor to do NeXT software. It's funny how a few bad quarters changes one's perspective. (If you're a developer who's had a bad experience with NeXT, maybe you should give it another chance.)

Conclusion

Around the time that Sun's engineering and scientific markets have dried up and Microsoft has sucked the marrow out of Silicon Graphics's bones, there will be a broad selection of productivity software for NeXT. Then, largely because of evangelism, NeXT will eclipse Sun as the dominant workstation manufacturer.

There's one more reason. Medicine will cure death, and government will repeal taxes before Steve will fail. You can quote me.

Ok. Ok. Ok. Ok. Ok. Joe Pesci saving a style change in PageMaker. (Paragraph rule options, Paragraph rules, Paragraph specifications, Edit Style, Define Styles.)

object-oriented A customer who always complains.

> *Object-oriented development systems will always make programming easier "next year."*

offsite The gathering of upper management at exotic places to discuss how to lay off people.

> *The "warm and fuzzies" produced by offsites in Santa Cruz wear off when you get to the intersection of Highways 17 and 280.*

"New versions of software only get 30% faster."

Ok. Ok. Ok. Ok. Ok. Joe Pesci saving a style change in PageMaker. (Paragraph rule options, Paragraph rules, Paragraph specifications, Edit Style, Define Styles.)

open architecture A hardware design that no one wants so you have to give it away.

optimization More than $3.00 per share.

order of magnitude How much every press release says a new version of software is going to be faster.

New versions of software only get 30% faster.

orphan A child whose parents use computers.

OSF Open Suckers Foundation.

overlap The part of a programmer's belly that hangs over his jeans.

oxymoron Anything that upsets the management of a company.

More on oxymorons...

The Top Ten Computer Oxymorons

10. Three-hour battery

9. Bug free

8. Upward compatibility

7. BusinessLand store

6. Apple management

5. Value-added reseller

4. Compaq margins

3. Microsoft upgrade

2. NeXT software

1. IBM innovation

PageMaker Proof that there is a God, and that He or She loves Apple Computer.

> *PageMaker is for wimps. QuarkXPress is for masochists.*

paradigm Anything an analyst believes you shifted.

parallel port Simultaneously adapting software to Macintosh and Windows.

parallel processing Hiring new bozos as you lay off old ones.

PARC Please Assume our Research Costs.

parity Ensuring that all vice presidents get the same kind of company car.

partition The only thing that separates employees from managers in egalitarian companies.

PC Politically Corrupt.

PDA Post Desktop Apple.

peripheral Anything a computer manufacturer doesn't think it can make money on.

Perot When your Macintosh unexpectedly quits and restarts.

pinhead A bozo with a crewcut.

"PageMaker is for wimps. QuarkXPress is for masochists."

PIP Product Introduction Plan. An internal Apple document circulated throughout the company to ensure that everyone approves of a product introduction.

> *Everyone signs PIPs without reading them.*

> *PIPs add two months to the delivery of a product.*

pirates College students.

plasma display What happens when clone manufacturers compete on price.

platform A $64 word for "computer" that is used to impress analysts and the press.

PMS Post Macintosh Syndrome. The feeling of IBM PC owners that they use the wrong computer. (PMS first appeared on January 24, 1984.)

"PIPs add two months to the delivery of a product."

port A four-letter word used to describe uninspired programming.

portables The children of nerds.

More on portables...

How to Tell If Your Child Will Use a Macintosh or a PC

You met your mate at a

a) Grateful Dead concert (Macintosh)

b) Wall Street analyst meeting (PC)

During pregnancy, you had a craving for

a) Jolt (Macintosh)

b) Spam and Velveeta on pumpernickel bread (PC)

During the ultrasound, you swear you heard the baby humming

   a) *In-a-Gadda-Da-Vida* (Macintosh)

   b) *Moon River* (PC)

When the water broke, you thought that

   a) Your Evian had spilled (Macintosh)

   b) Your 300 SL's roof was leaking (PC)

Your child's stroller was built by

   a) Lexus (Macintosh)

   b) Martha Stewart (PC)

Your child craved

   a) More RAM (Macintosh)

   b) A faster processor (PC)

Your child stopped playing with blocks after

   a) Realizing that the blocks had a monospace font (Macintosh)

   b) Your child still hasn't stopped playing with blocks (PC)

PostScript The royalty stream from Apple Computer to Adobe Systems. See also *Display PostScript* and *Encapsulated PostScript*.

PowerBook A device that ruined more marriages than sex, drugs, and alcohol, and saved more marriages than M. Scott Peck. (The problem is no one can predict what effect it will have on *your* marriage.)

The less time you have before your flight takes off, the more time it takes to shut down your PowerBook.

Your PowerBook's hard disk will die immediately after your plane takes off, or right before you save a file because you're landing.

If you can hear your PowerBook's hard disk in an airplane, it's about to die.

Apple uses one more size torx screw in a PowerBook than you have torx screw drivers.

Apple uses one more torx screw in a PowerBook than you can find.

PowerBook batteries last half as long as Apple says they will last.

Even more on PowerBooks...

The Five Best Names for a PowerBook Utilities Package

5. LUMP: LeVitus Utilities for the Macintosh PowerBook

4. DUMP: Dvorak Utilities for the Macintosh PowerBook

3. BUMP: Bobker Utilities for the Macintosh PowerBook[1]

2. SUMP: Sculley Utilities for the Macintosh PowerBook

1. GRUMP: Guy's Remarkable Utilities for the Macintosh PowerBook

---

[1] Thanks to Andrew Carol.

122   PowerBook

The Top Five Alternatives to Apple's PowerBook Advertising Tag Line ("It's the next thing.")

5. It's light and Compaq for you.

4. It's Dell to travel without one.

3. It's the Zenith of portability.[1]

2. It's indispensable when you're Outbound.

1. It's the International Business Machine.

Power PC Abbreviation for "The Power of Political Correctness," that is, the desire of Apple to gain legitimacy by allying with IBM.

power user Someone with more than 25 fonts.

> *Three-fourths of the fonts in your Macintosh are not used.*

> *The more fonts in a document, the less content it has.*

prenuptial Deciding who gets the 170 and who gets the IIci.

print merge A command in Microsoft Word that enables you to create personalized letters for people you don't know, about things they don't care about, with addresses they're no longer at.

printing What pen-based computer companies hope everyone wants to do on a computer.

> *A printer only crashes when printing documents you haven't saved.*

"The more fonts in a document, the less content it has."

[1] Thanks to Alan Spurgeon.

A fax modem only crashes when faxing documents you haven't saved.

privileges All the orange juice and first-class tickets you want.

product manager A person who has all the responsibility but none of the power.

programmer A person who has all the power but claims to have none of the responsibility.

Each time you remove one programmer from a project, you reduce development time by one month.

The optimal number of programmers on a project is three: one to create the architecture, one to design the interface, and one that understands the architecture and interface in case the other two quit.

For still more about programming, see "If You Want to Program," at the end of this chapter.

programmer switch Someone who transfers from a Macintosh to a Windows development team.

progress indicator Going public.

prompt Releasing a bug-fix version of software before *MacWEEK*, *InfoWorld*, or *PCWeek* writes a story about the bugs.

protectionism Preventing a Japanese company from selling its product at an American company's manufacturing price.

prototype Anything that helps a company get venture capital.

"A fax modem only crashes when faxing documents you haven't saved."

PS/2 [Too late and] Pretty Sad, Two.

public domain software Software from companies that cannot afford to prosecute pirates.

publish and subscribe Editors of a magazine getting a subscription sent to their home because the office copy gets stolen.

pundit Someone who cannot do and cannot write.

> *Macintosh pundits and press act like their name sounds; for example, Winer, Gassée, Crabb, and Borrell.*

"Macintosh pundits and press act like their name sounds; for example, Winer, Gassée, Crabb, and Borrell."

More on programming...

If You Want To Program

Reprinted from *MacUser* April 1992

Brenda Ueland probably never used a Macintosh. She may have never used a personal computer at all. Nevertheless, her book, *If You Want to Write*, is the best book about programming ever written.

Ueland, a writer, editor, and teacher, died in 1985 at the age of 93. Too bad—I think she would have loved to write with a Macintosh. You've probably never heard of her unless you are a writer. (If you're a writer and you haven't heard of her, something is wrong with you.)

This column explains how to apply her principles of writing to programming. I hope this is okay with her, and that she forgives me if it's not. I have a feeling, however, that she's Up There, smiling. If you're not a writer or a programmer, you should buy her book anyway to help you get through life.

I have a selfish motive. People often send me software, because they think that their product is going to blow me away and compel me to write a column about it. Dream on. Ninety-nine percent of the software I receive is not worth booting. I donate most of this stuff to my church. Companies can save me a lot of trouble by sending their software directly to Menlo Park Presbyterian Church, 950 Santa Cruz Ave., Menlo Park, CA 94025; attention: Walt Gerber.

Seldom as it occurs, when I do see software I love, I call the company and try to buy a piece of the firm and perhaps get a seat on the board of directors. I call this the Guy's Golden Touch Investment algorithm: "Whatever is gold, Guy touches." I've touched only three programs so far. I don't want to touch any more, but the Macintosh market could use a shot of innovation.

Talent and Originality

Ueland's book begins with a chapter entitled, "Everybody is talented, original and has something to say." It ends with a chapter entitled, "'He whose face gives no light shall never become a star'—William Blake." Get the idea? Her book is about creativity, freedom, integrity, and courage in writing (and programming).

Her book is for aspiring writers and the aspiring writer in all of us. It is not for prissy, self-centered, "successful" writers who have convinced themselves that they know it all and who are trying to convince others that writing is for the intellectually elite. She in-courages writers—literally putting the courage in writers—to break the "oughts" of writing and to find ways to express themselves.

In the same sense, this column is for aspiring programmers and the aspiring programmer in all of us. It is not for prissy, self-centered "successful" programmers who have convinced themselves that they know it all and who are trying to convince others that programming is for the technically elite. I want to in-courage programmers to break the shackles of what software reviewers, Apple, and Macintosh think programs ought to be.

How to Program

There are three kinds of Macintosh software today: incremental upgrades of existing programs; incremental rip-offs of existing programs; and bizarre, touristy drek that should be sold in hotel gift shops. All three are the products of either small minds or big minds constrained.

If development of these kinds of software continues, Macintosh will be slimed by the Peter Principle of Computing: a computer rises to the level of the incompetence of its programmers. The only way to stop and reverse the Peter Principle is to listen to what Ueland has to say. Here is what she would tell you if she were alive and if she were a programmer:

Program freely. Have rollicking fun when you program. Program as if you were creating something for your friends. Make programming easy on and interesting to yourself, without fear of failure. Thumb your nose at the know-it-alls, critics, managers, and MBAs at least once a month, and program freely.

Program recklessly. Ignore "market" requirements (the market usually doesn't know what it wants until it sees it). Go where no programmer has gone before. Add

Excel, PageMaker, and RTF compatibility at the end. If ever. If you want to. Make history, not compatibility. Your goal is to create software so great that customers are willing to rekey data, so tell the world to kiss your SCSI port and go for it.

Program for love. Programming is generosity. You have an insight or know a truth about how a computer can do something. You want other people to share it. So you program. Put your love for people into your program. It will touch people, and all of you will be the better for it. It may even sell—because people are willing to buy love on a disk. (If you want to see love on a disk, look at HAM, from Microseeds Publishing. This little jewel allows you to customize the order of your Apple menu and it adds a folder to the Apple menu containing a directory of the items used recently. HAM shows some serious love of System 7 users.)

Program honestly. Most software is dishonest. When you look at it, you can't believe that a programmer with a triple-digit IQ believes that this is the way things should work. Instead, the software is saying, "This isn't really what I think. The design specs said to do it this way." Or, "My boss saw John Sculley demo a HyperCard stack that had this kind of interface." Or, "My boss saw this feature in an Apple video." Be honest. And be accepted or rejected on what you really believe.

Program to infect. Great software leaps from a computer and infects people's brains. It makes their fingertips sizzle and mouse buttons palpitate. Infection happens immediately or it doesn't happen at all. It won't happen because people try-and-try to like the program or because a reviewer says it's good. As you program, keep the goal of infection in mind.

Program for intrinsic rewards. Programming yields two intrinsic rewards. First, programming helps you understand your feelings better. Nothing forces a person to understand himself better than trying to communicate his feelings. Second, programming increases creativity: the more you use your creative power, the more you will have. (Don't you wish PowerBook batteries worked this way?) No matter how many copies of your program you sell, if you program for intrinsic rewards, you'll reap satisfaction.

Program in the present. To borrow a Ueland analogy, work like a child stringing beads: one bead at a time, unconcerned about what the necklace might look like with different beads. Ignore the rumors you read in *MacWEEK* about DAL, RISC chips, and cross-platform compilers. Instead, do the best you can with the present. If you wait for the perfect platform and the perfect object-oriented compiler, you may never finish anything. Create a product so great that people won't care about upgrading to the latest gee-whiz-what-have-we-shipped-but-not-perfected technology.

Program anything you want. Ueland quotes William Blake to illustrate this point: "Better to strangle an infant in its cradle than nurse unacted desires." Ignore the forecast about market size in the year 2000 and the competitive analysis of the viability of various platforms. Tackle anything that fascinates you: a product for NeXT, an Excel killer—even a Macintosh database program. If your company won't let you do this, then quit. Have you ever met anyone who regretted quitting a job?

Program microscopically. Take a close look at the software you've created. Does it show a microscopic attention to detail? A fine eye? Empathy for the user? Forget "patentable, paradigm-shifting algorithms for the '90s" because great software comes down to minute details. Get out your microscope and program software for mortals.

If you want to see products not programmed microscopically, look at Microsoft Word or Aldus PageMaker. Don't you love dialog boxes that contain three pop-up menus and nine buttons (Save, Cancel, Apply, Set Default, Apply Set, Apply Default, Default Apply, Default Set, and Default Default) plus four buttons leading to additional dialogs?

These products were programmed with a telescope. It must have something to do with being from the Pacific Northwest. Maybe there are hooded owls living in Word and PageMaker, so it is against the law to cut down the number of dialog boxes.

Program when you are discouraged. Ueland quotes Van Gogh: "If you hear a voice within you saying: You are no painter, then paint by all means, lad, and that voice will be silenced, but only by working." No one—not Andy Hertzfeld, Bill Atkinson, Steve Capps, or Michael Jordan—woke up one day and was great. They make it look easy because they've worked hard. Great programming is opening up a vein and pouring blood into a disk.

Or Your Money Back

In a rare moment of humility, let me tell you that I haven't done Ueland's book justice. If you are interested in programming or working with programmers, run, do not walk, to your nearest bookstore and buy *If You Want to Write*. It is one of the few books I have read more than five times. I have so much faith in Ueland's book that if you buy it and it doesn't help you, I will give you your money back. I won't even say that about *my* books.

Here's the information you need to find it: *If You Want to Write* (ISBN 0-915308-94-0) by Brenda Ueland, Graywolf Press, 2402 University Ave. Suite 203, Saint Paul, Minnesota 55114, (612) 641-0077, (612) 641-0036 fax, $8.95 plus shipping.

And please don't send me your software unless you think Ueland would like it, because my church's hard disks are almost full.[2]

[2] My mother hated this column because she thought I was mean to tell people not to send me their software. On the other hand, she has not seen the software people send me.

Quadra A version of Macintosh that is incompatible with four times more software than any other Macintosh.

Quadra A version of Macintosh that is incompatible with four times more software than any other Macintosh.

Que A line of faxes waiting to be printed in Carmel, Indiana.

>*Read any book Robin Williams writes.*

>*The Macintosh is not a typewriter so there is one space between sentences.*

For still more about Que, see "Anything is Possible," at the end of this chapter.

QuickDraw The belief that the world is nothing more than little regions clipped together.

QuickTime The HyperCard of the '90s.

More on Que...

Anything Is Possible

Reprinted from *MacUser* January 1992

Copyright © 1992, Ziff Communications Company

The house is an hour north of the Golden Gate Bridge in a town called Santa Rosa. It is the kind of place that only your parents would like: a quaint downtown with little restaurants and antique shops. It's not a real city, because it doesn't have a Fry's Electronics or a Price Club or a ComputerWare. Most people would stop there only if they needed gas. You wouldn't *go* to Santa Rosa.

The house is 750 square feet. It has two bedrooms, two closets, no garage, and no backyard. It's rented. Four people live in it: mother, daughter (age 5), and two sons (ages 9 and 13). She is a single parent, and people often ask her if being a single mother of three is difficult. She replies, "Yes, but it's easier than being married and a single mother of four."

She supports her family primarily by writing books about Macintosh. When the kids are asleep, she steals a chair from the kitchen and takes it to her workroom—which is also her bedroom. Her Macintosh is on the left side of the bed. Her scanner is on top of her sewing machine. Her mousepad is on the bed, because there isn't enough space next to her Macintosh. Hermann Miller would have a coronary in this work space.

The bed is high off the floor, and she built it herself. She built it high—three feet, to be precise—so that her LaserWriter could fit underneath. Space in her house is at a premium. When she works, she can't spread too many things out on her bed, because it would disturb her daughter, who is sleeping on the far side. Her daughter is sleeping there because she outgrew the old bed that was under the desk in the boys' room.

Beware: T Square

She was teaching typography and design at Santa Rosa Junior College when Apple introduced Macintosh. She and her T square and rubber cement resisted computers until one of her students brought over his Macintosh and left it on her kitchen table for a week. She connected with it quickly. She borrowed a Macintosh from the college for the summer. Later she took out a loan to buy an SE.

She quit teaching typography and started teaching HyperCard and Microsoft Works classes for the business department. The college let her work only part-time, so she had to hold several part-time jobs. One was designing box covers for hard-core porn flicks. (She insists that she took this job to learn the four-color-printing process.) Mainly, though, she taught Macintosh classes, and her class handouts grew into a little book. People from other classes asked for it. The county wanted to buy a dozen for its employees.

A small publisher in Oregon gave her a contract to write a HyperCard book. This was the deal she got: no advance and 11-percent royalties for camera-ready art. (Most authors get 15-percent royalties and provide only text.) While the publisher was reading two early chapters, she finished her little book about Macintosh basics. Later she realized that her publisher wasn't doing enough for her, so she studied how to self-publish a book.

When her father died, he left her mother some money. She borrowed $15,000 from her mother and started a company to publish her books. She finished her books on her

SE and printed 5,000 copies of *Macintosh Basics: An informal guide to using the Macintosh* and 2,000 copies of *The Mac is not a typewriter: A style manual for creating professional-level type on your Macintosh.*

Berkeley *Marketing* User Group

She forced herself to go to the BMUG booth at the 1989 Seybold Conference. She met Robert Lettieri of BMUG and told him that she'd like BMUG to look at the books. His reply was, "Great! We love to read Macintosh books. We rip 'em to shreds. We haven't found a book we like yet. Arthur Naiman tried to give us 30 copies of *The Macintosh Bible,* and we told him to take them back."

With trepidation, she gave him a copy of each book. The next day, Harry Critchfield from BMUG called and told her that he loved them. When she hung up, she cried. A few weeks later, Jerry Whiting reviewed *The Mac is not a typewriter* in *Aldus Magazine* and told people to buy it. The magazine didn't list a phone number for her, and her company wasn't listed in the phone directory, because she couldn't afford a business line.

The books started selling. She went back to BMUG and, after the meeting, had dinner with the core group. They gave her ideas about how to market her books. Scott Kronick gave her the name and address of Arthur Naiman. She wrote to him. She never heard from him. (I contacted Naiman's office about publishing *The Macintosh Way,* and his secretary told me that "Mr. Naiman only publishes his own books." Funny how the world works....)

Kronick also gave a BMUG member named Kimn Neilson copies of the books, and Kimn offered to show the books to Peachpit Press. Twenty-four hours after he got them, Ted Nace, the president of Peachpit Press, called and offered to publish *Macintosh Basics*. After some convincing, he also acquired *The Mac is not a typewriter*.

The rest, to use a cliché, is history. *Macintosh Basics* became *The Little Mac Book*. *The Mac is not a typewriter* remained *The Mac is not a typewriter*. They've each sold more than 50,000 copies. The author is Robin Williams, and she's now applying for a loan to buy a house for herself and her three kids after years of making $9,000 to $12,000.

Happily Ever After

The End. Happily ever after, right? Wrong.

Nine months after Peachpit Press, one of the littlest book publishers, published *The Little Mac Book,* Que Corp., one of the biggest book publishers, published a book called *The Little Mac Book.*

Did Que intentionally and maliciously steal the idea? No. Que had already published a book called *The Big Mac Book,* and its *The Little Mac Book* was to be a complementary volume. Que's rationale was probably this: Because we didn't steal the name and we had plans to do one before Robin's book appeared, we can go ahead with a book of the same name.

Could Peachpit sue Que? Maybe. Book titles are not copyrightable, but there are issues of unfair competition here. It doesn't really matter, though, because the cost and hassle of litigation eliminate the *practicality* of legal actions. Still, people are going into bookstores to buy Robin's *The Little Mac Book,* and they're getting Que's *The Little Mac Book.*

This bothers Robin a great deal. She wrote a letter to Que but never sent it. Here's a paragraph from it:

"There is nothing I can do about your undermining the sales of my book. There is nothing I can do about your riding on the wave of my book's popularity. There is nothing I can do about the people who read the reviews and think they are buying my book and get yours instead. There is nothing I can do about the fact that you will seriously affect my livelihood that I have struggled so hard to create. There is nothing I can do except tell you that I don't think you are very nice. It won't change anything, and it doesn't even really make me feel any better, but I have to say it. You are not very nice."

Robin is wrong. There is always something you can do. You could, for example, tell me. I, in turn, will tell 375,000 readers of *MacUser*. Then we can make Robin's Little Macintosh Problem into a cause and show a big company that we Macintosh crazies are a potent force. We can show them that they should do the right thing the right way and rename their *The Little Mac Book*.

Name That Book

I spoke to Que's publisher, Lloyd Short. He seemed like a reasonable person. Actually, I wish I could tell you that he wasn't, so that I could unleash the wrath of Macintosh on him. I just think that he needs to be *motivated*—if you catch my drift.

This is what I want you to do: Send him a fax at (317) 573-2583 or a letter to 11711 N. College Avenue, Carmel, IN 46032. In your fax or letter, insist that this situation be corrected and then give him your suggestion for a new name for his book. Also, go to your bookstores and tell them this story and make sure that they sell the right *The Little Mac Book*. Poor Lloyd—I hope he has a lot of fax paper.

Don't read this as a purely negative story. Take delight in the fact that an unemployed single mother of three on welfare pursued her dream of writing and publishing cool Macintosh books, that she ultimately achieved success and popularity, and that she helped tens of thousands of people use their Macintoshes better.

And that at the height of her success, she was "wronged" by a company and that the Macintosh community rose to the challenge, defended her, and made things right.

One more thing: If you ever get a letter from a unknown single mother of three on welfare who wants you to publish her book, you should respond. In the Macintosh world, anything is possible.

(P.S. In all fairness, you should know that one of Robin's part-time jobs was doing layout for After Hours, a software company that I have an interest in, and that Peachpit Press also publishes a book that I wrote.)[1]

[Publisher's note: This issue is over a year old and has been resolved. To prevent any confusion going forward, Que changed the title of its book to Que's Little Mac Book, *and this was deemed an amicable solution by all concerned. This once and for all closed the book on the Little Mac issue, so please don't fax Lloyd Short any more motivational messages.]*

[1] I've spoken to groups in Santa Rosa three times since this column appeared, and they did not like my description of their beautiful, fascinating, worth-driving-to-from-Alaska city.

reality distortion The ability of Steve Jobs to make people buy a computer that doesn't have software.

ragged right The Republican party.

radio buttons The multiple-choice quiz of the '90s.

RAM Really Aggravating Marketing.

> *Double the amount of RAM Apple says is required to run any version of the System.*

RAM page What virtual memory goes on when it thrashes inefficiently.[1]

---

[1] Thanks to Andrew Carol.

redeployment A layoff that doesn't affect a company's stock price.

ReadMeFirst A list of bugs that didn't get fixed.

read only What software companies wish their customers would do when they want technical support. For even more on reading, see, "How to Read a Macintosh Magazine," at the end of this chapter.

real time Answering technical-support questions within four hours.

real world "Software is slow, late, expensive, and buggy."

reality distortion The ability of Steve Jobs to make people buy a computer that doesn't have software.

registered owners The first people to buy a product and the last to get it upgraded.

relational database Any database that's hard to use, slow, and sells in small volumes.

ResEdit Ginsu knife for nerds.

résumé The only reason an MS-DOS bigot will use a Macintosh.

> **Never** hire @ *person* who uses **more** than *two* **fonts** in **a** *résumé*✎

return key What polite people do after using the rest room.

reviewer A person who can use a word processor but not a compiler.

rich text format Bill Gates' prenuptial agreement.

right justify Orrin Hatch's and Arlen Specter's favorite style of formatting.

ROTFL Resting On The Foresight of Lawyers.

RTFM Read The Fulfilling Manual.

> *If people read manuals, half the technical support staff would be unemployed.*

ruler Partner-level venture capitalist.

run About all you can expect of software that shipped right before Macworld Expo.

More on reading...

How to Read a Macintosh Magazine

First published in *MacHome Journal* Sneak Preview Edition

The people who publish this magazine tell me it's targeted at first-time and novice Macintosh users. You may not be familiar with how Macintosh magazines work, so this column is going to give you the inside scoop and explain how to read a Macintosh magazine.

1. Understand who's running the joint. The world can be divided into two groups: those who can do and those who can't. Those who can do, start companies like Apple and Microsoft and become zillionaires. Those who can't do and can write become freelancers, reviewers, columnists, and editors. (Those who can't do and can't write become Wall Street financial analysts.)

   Thus, whatever you read is tainted by the envy of not being able to do and not being rewarded for not being able to do. I've been on both sides: trust me, it is easier for a programmer to write a good

"If people read manuals, half the technical support staff would be unemployed."

review than a reviewer to write a good program. Macintosh magazines are no more than one data point in the selection of products, so ask friends, geeks, and user group members what they recommend. Don't act on only what you read.

2. Don't believe the rating systems. Macintosh magazines assign numerical ratings with a number of stars or mice: the more stars or mice, the better the product. These ratings mean as much as the metals of military dictators, and you should consider them as significant to determine "goodness."

The problem is that products are rated by different people at different times for different needs. Thus, if you were choosing between two word processors, the one with five mice is not necessarily better than the one with four. The reviewers are probably different, the ratings may be for the latest version of one and a prior version of another, and your needs may be different from what the product does. That is, a five-mice word processor for a writer is different than a five-mice word processor for a business person.

3. Don't believe the awards. Every year Macintosh magazines hold grandiose award ceremonies because the spouses of the publishers own catering companies. The awards are often flawed in two ways: first, some are given for the best new product in a category. Often, there are few new products in a category, so it's easy to win. Imagine if car magazines picked the best new sports car instead of simply the best sports car: what do you care when the car was introduced? You want the best sports car at the time.

Second, the categories are flawed. Sometimes I scratch my head and wonder why an outline processor and a contact manager are competing in the "information management" category. This is like choosing between *Terminator II* and *Fried Green Tomatoes* in the action-film category because both had scenes in which large vehicles (a truck in *Terminator II* and a train in *Fried Green Tomatoes*) nearly killed or killed a young boy.

4. The mail order ads don't indicate what are the best-selling or highest-quality products. Many people look at mail order ads and think, "Ah, MacCollection is advertising Megalosoft WordMaker. It must be the best word processor." Guess again. The mail order ads are paid for by the software companies. All it takes to be in these ads is a little green.

5. Conflicts of interest are more plentiful than face lifts in Beverly Hills. I, of all people, need to tell you this. If Macintosh magazines prevented people with conflicts of interest from writing, there would be nothing but mail order ads and liars. (If only stars without face lifts could act, every film would be animated.) This practice is radically different from most of the magazines and newspapers you read— *The New York Times*, for example—where conflicts of interest are forbidden.

It comes down to this: Macintosh magazines use many freelance writers and do not pay them enough to do nothing except write for the magazine. (Instead the magazines throw $100,000 Macworld Expo parties to impress their competition.) The author of the article may be a consultant to the company (or competitor), own stock in the company (or competitor), or is in some way beholden to the company (or competitor).

Often the people who can best write about products often have conflicts of interest. For example, unarguably, the best person to write a review of a database is a database consultant. This person is also likely to depend on referrals from the database companies for consulting leads. This system is okay as long as you know how it works.

There you have it: how to read Macintosh magazines. I hope you've enjoyed this column because it may mean I'll never "eat lunch in this town again." On the other hand, I may be end up as regular columnist on this page of *MacHome Journal*. If I do, there's one more piece of advice for reading Macintosh magazines: always start from the back page.[2]

---

[2]Sorry, I ended up not writing for *Mac Home Journal*.

More on reading ...

search What Borland makes the police do to its competitors.

sabbatical Preparation time for getting laid off.

SAM Strategic Alliance Meshugas.

SANE Simply Another Numeric Environment.[1]

scanner Someone who goes to a retail store to look at software and then buys it from a mail-order company.

SCSI The Macintosh Orifice.

SCSI chain The string of people you have to talk to when calling a software company for technical support.[2]

---

[1] Some people think that SANE stands for Standard Apple Numerics Environment. However, doesn't "standard" imply predominance and consistency?

---

[2] Thanks to John Holland.

search What Borland makes the police do to its competitors.

serial What EtherNet eats for breakfast.

seniority Going through two reorganizations.

> *After you go through three reorganizations at Apple, you get to be a manager.*

server Software that enables other people to crash your computer.

shareware Software not good enough to sell but not bad enough to give away.

shift-click Switching from a Macintosh to a NeXT. See also *click*.

Silicon Forest Bill Gates's backyard.

Silicon Tubes The place American chip manufacturers tell Congress they are going unless they get trade barriers.

Silicon Plains Fargo, North Dakota, the home of Great Plains Software. (Prior to Great Plains, the most exciting thing in Fargo was $5 blackjack at the Holiday Inn.)

Silicon Valley An area in California where "leverage" is a verb and "desktop" is an adjective.

More on Silicon Valley...

The Five Best License Plates in Silicon Valley

5. Bill Gates   COPY MAC

"After you go through three reorganizations at Apple, you get to be a manager."

4.	John Sculley	SUE BILL
3.	Steve Jobs	NO SFTWR
2.	Jean-Louis Gassée	GRN CARD
1.	Beth Kawasaki	NO EMAIL

SIMM Send In More Money!

SINC Single Income, No Clones.

single density An MBA working by himself or herself. See also *double density*.

site license Employees giving software to their friends and family without fear of legal repercussion.

smilies Emotions for nerds.

> For still more on smilies, see "The Unofficial Smilie Dictionary," at the end of this chapter.

sneaker net Distributing files by Just Doing It.

SoftPC Catsup on chateaubriand.

software library A pirate's hard disk.

> *Software that comes in black boxes is hard to use.*
>
> *Software that comes in white boxes is wimpy.*

spiff A payoff made to computer salesmen to encourage them to sell you stuff you don't need.

spike Initial sales for vaporware.

stack How much you have to read in order to use an IBM PC.

state-of-the-art An expensive product that isn't selling.

> *"Software that comes in black boxes is hard to use."*

strategic Anything that loses money.

StuffIt What Steve Jobs would like to tell John Sculley.

suit A person, typically in management, who believes in formality, standardization, and rigidity. Antonym: T-shirt.

> *One suit can negate the work of twenty t-shirts.*

Sun An ancient icon worshipped by lost people.

superstore A store that doesn't provide service and support but doesn't charge for them.

surge protector A condom for computers.

sysop Someone with too much time on his or her hands.

System heap The dump where IBM disposed of the unsold PC JRs.

system software Whatever Apple says it is, whatever Microsoft copies, and whatever IBM envies.

> *Wait nine months until you convert to a new version of the System.*

"Wait nine months until you convert to a new version of the System."

More on smilies...

The Unofficial Smilie Dictionary

By Donald Daybell

Like prehistoric cave dwellers, the devotees of electronic bulletin-boards and E-mail have struggled to find a new way to express themselves. Wall painting would not work. Words, it seems, are not enough. Inarticulate sounds cannot be displayed on screens. To make their messages feel more like personal contact, they have hit on using the punctuation marks on an ordinary keyboard in order to pull faces at each other. To read these signs, you have to put your head on your left shoulder.

The basic unit is:

`: - )`

The "smilie," a standard smiling face. In context, this can mean "I'm happy to hear from you," or other pleasantries. The smilie can also wink:

`; - )`

or frown:

`: - (`

among other things. The language can express many things about the user's appearance:

`8 - )   : - { )   8 : - )   : - ) - 8   : - Q   @ : - )`

These signs mean, respectively, that the user wears sunglasses, has a mustache, is a little girl, is a big girl, smokes, wears a turban.

The smilie can also indicate some subtleties of mood and response:

`: - D   : - /   : - e   : - 7   : - X`

These mean that he is laughing, is skeptical, is disappointed, is wry, is keeping his lips sealed.

Many of the signs (perhaps the majority in use on America's biggest computer networks) are simply absurd fun, verging on the unintelligible:

`: - F   * : o )   + - : - )   @ =`

The user is a buck-toothed vampire with one tooth missing, is a clown, holds religious office, is pro-nuclear.

More on smilies...

: -)	Your basic smilie. This smilie is used to inflect a sarcastic or joking statement since we can't hear voice inflection over UNIX.
; -)	Winky smilie. User just made a flirtatious and/or sarcastic remark. More of a "don't hit me for what I just said" smilie.
: - (	Frowning smilie. User did not like that last statement or is upset or depressed about something.
: - I	Indifferent smilie. Better than a frowning smilie but not quite as good as a happy smilie.
: - >	User just made a really biting sarcastic remark. Worse than a : -).
; - >	Winky and devil combined. A very lewd remark was just made.

Those are the basic ones... Here are some somewhat less common ones:

(- :	User is left handed
% -)	User has been staring at a green screen for 15 hours straight
: *)	User is drunk
[:]	User is a robot
8 -)	User is wearing sunglasses
B : -)	Sunglasses on head
: : -)	User wears normal glasses
B -)	User wears horn-rimmed glasses
8 : -)	User is a little girl
: -) - 8	User is a big girl

: - {)	User has a mustache
: - { }	User wears lipstick
{ : -)	User wears a toupee
} : - (	Toupee in an updraft
: - [	User is a vampire
: - E	Bucktoothed vampire
: - F	Bucktoothed vampire with one tooth missing
: - 7	User just made a wry statement
: -) ~	User drools
: - ~)	User has a cold
: ' - (	User is crying
: ' -)	User is so happy, s/he is crying
: - @	User is screaming
: - #	User wears braces
: ^)	User has a broken nose
: v)	User has a broken nose, but it's the other way
: _)	User's nose is sliding off of his face
: <)	User is from an Ivy League school
: - &	User is tongue tied
= : -)	User is a hosehead
- : -)	User is a punk rocker
- : - (	(real punk rockers don't smile)
: =)	User has two noses
+ - : -)	User is the pope or holds some other religious office

`':-)`	User shaved one of his eyebrows off this morning
`,:-)`	Same thing, other side
`¦-I`	User is asleep
`¦-O`	User is yawning/snoring
`:-Q`	User is a smoker
`:-?`	User smokes a pipe
`O-)`	Megaton Man On Patrol! (or else, user is a scuba diver)
`O :-)`	User is an angel (at heart, at least)
`:-S`	User just made an incoherent statement
`:-D`	User is laughing (at you!)
`:-C`	User is really bummed
`:-/`	User is skeptical
`C=:-)`	User is a chef
`@=`	User is pro-nuclear war
`*<:-)`	User is wearing a Santa Claus Hat
`:-o`	Uh oh!
`(8-o`	It's Mr. Bill!
`*:o)`	And Bozo the Clown!
`3:]`	Pet smilie
`3:[`	Mean Pet smilie
`d8=`	Your pet beaver is wearing goggles and a hard hat.
`:-9`	User is licking his/her lips
`%-6`	User is braindead

More on smilies...

[: -)	User is wearing a walkman
(: I	User is an egghead
K : P	User is a little kid with a propeller beanie
@ : -)	User is wearing a turban
: - Ø	No Yelling! (Quiet Lab)
: - :	Mutant Smilie
	The invisible smilie
. -)	User only has one eye
, -)	Ditto...but he's winking
X - (	User just died
C=}>;*{))	Mega-Smilie... A drunk, devilish chef with a toupee in an updraft, a mustache, and a double chin

Note: A lot of these can be typed without noses to make midget smilies.

:)	Midget smilie
:]	Gleep...a friendly midget smilie who will gladly be your friend
=)	Variation on a theme...
: D	Laughter
: I	Hmmm...
: (	Sad
: [	Real Downer
: O	Yelling
: , (	Crying

[ ]	Hugs and
: *	Kisses
¦ I	Asleep
¦ ^ o	Snoring
: - '	smilie spitting out its chewing tobacco
: - 1	smilie bland face
: - # ¦	smilie face with bushy mustache
: - $	smilie face with its mouth wired shut
: - 6	smilie after eating something sour
: - *	smilie after eating something bitter
(: - (	unsmilie frowning
(: -)	smilie big-face
) : - (	unsmilie big-face
: - t	cross smilie
: - p	smilie sticking its tongue out (at you!)
: - [	un-smilie blockhead
: -]	smilie blockhead
: - a	lefty smilely touching tongue to nose
: - d	lefty smilie razzing you
g -)	smilie with pince-nez glasses
: - j	left-smiling smilely
: - x	"my lips are sealed" smilie
: - c	bummed out smilie
: - v	talking head smilie
: - /	lefty undecided smilie
. -]	one-eyed smilely

More on smilies...

, -}	wry and winking
: -=)	older smilie with mustache
:u)	smilie with funny-looking left nose
:n)	smilie with funny-looking right nose
:<	midget unsmilie
:>	midget smilie
~~:-(	net.flame
8 :-I	net.unix-wizards
X-(	net.suicide
E-:-I	net.ham-radio
>:-I	net.startrek
3:o[	net.pets
:-}	beard
:-X	bow tie
<:I	dunce
:-8(	condescending stare
:-(	Drama
:-)	Comedy
:-o	Surprise
8-¦	Suspense
:-	Male
>-	Female
¦-O	Birth
8-#	Death
8	Infinity

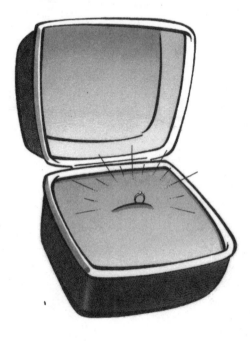

Token ring A diamond ring of less than 2.0 carats for the wife of a computer owner.

T-shirt A person, typically not in management, who believes in egalitarianism, change, and innovation. Antonym: suit.

tab-delimited Limiting how many drinks a person can buy on credit.

TeachText The Macintosh application with the largest installed base.

technical support The difference between the cost of blank diskettes and the retail price of software.

The Three Best Tech Support Stories I Ever Heard

3. A customer had a problem printing a file and called Aldus' technical support department. Unable to solve the problem on the phone, the technical support person asked the customer to "send in a copy of the file." A week later a *photocopy* of the disk arrived.

2. A customer toting a young boy brought in her Macintosh to Tom Zorn in Eugene, Oregon complaining that her floppy drive didn't work. Tom opened the Macintosh up and found two credit cards in the drive. (The customer didn't even know they were gone.)

   He told the customer that her son must have put the cards in the drive. She responded, "He knows that floppy disks go in there." Tom handed a credit card to the boy and asked, "Where does this go?" and the boy put it in the disk drive.

1. A customer complained to a Macintosh software company that its product was losing data and corrupting files. The company could not figure out why this was happening, so it sent someone to check the customer's Macintosh and watch how the customer used the product.

   The tech support person determined that nothing was wrong with the Macintosh and watched the customer all day but did not see the customer do anything that could have caused the problem. At the end of the day, the customer said, "See? I haven't done anything wrong," quit the application, and pinned the data diskette to a steel cabinet with a magnet.

I swear these are true stories.

For still more on tech support, see "Help!," at the end of this chapter.

template 1. Get venture capital. 2. Demo vaporware. 3. Go public.

test drive kit A demo version of software intended to convince people to buy something they don't need, from people they don't trust, with money they don't have.

Three Rules of Life Back up your hard disk. Rebuild your desktop. Send in your registration card.

> *If you adhere to only one of the Three Rules of Life, you're better than 90% of computer users.*

Token ring A diamond ring of less than 2.0 carats for the wife of a computer owner.

> *A woman's diamond ring should be 1 carat for each computer her fiancé owns.*

TouchBASE A royalty stream.

trade barrier A business practice that perpetuates inferior products in the name of patriotism.

Trojan horse Desktop publishing.

TrueType Software that never existed that was used to force Adobe to reduce PostScript license fees.

"A woman's diamond ring should be 1 carat for each computer her fiancé owns."

tweak A person who is never satisfied with the status quo and always sees ways to make the world a better place.

More on technical support...

Help!

Reprinted from *MacUser,* March, 1992

The most common kind of electronic mail message I receive is about how hard it is to get good technical support from Macintosh hardware and software companies. The messages are from two types of people: first, the exasperated souls who have already talked to the companies to no avail and think that I'm a technical guru who knows all the answers, and second, the aggravated souls who think that I'm going to intercede on their behalf and call the president of the company to get a remedy. (If this fails, I'm expected to write a nasty column about the company and humiliate the jerks forever.) I've got news for both types: I'm neither a technical guru nor a gun for hire.

When I get one of these messages, my dark side is tempted to respond by saying, "Why are you bugging me? This isn't my problem. Fight your own battle. I left ACIUS two years ago. Bill Gates doesn't listen to me. Fred Ebrahimi couldn't care less who I am. I haven't talked to Paul Brainerd in years. When I see John Warnock, I'm going to ask him for some fonts for myself—not help you."

But I don't. I'm a wimp. I'm afraid to. My light side refuses to abdicate control. I have nightmares that someone will read my response aloud at a user group meeting or print it in a newsletter. Or that someone will burn his copy of *The Macintosh Way* on CNN. (If you're going to burn one of my books on national television, please, for publicity's sake burn *Selling the Dream*.)

This column explains how to get good technical support. When it is published, my light side may let my dark side answer my E-mail. Or, my light side may simply refer you to this column in a one-line response that's stored in a Thunder 7 glossary—making a response accessible by pressing one function key.

Before You Call

Send in the registration card. On a bozo scale of 1 to 10, not sending in the registration card is a 9. The first thing most companies do when you ask for technical support is look you up in their database of registered customers. If you're not there, you're starting off on the wrong foot, because the support person is thinking, "Is this a pirate or not?"

Registering lets you to take the moral high ground. If a company doesn't send you notices of upgrades or new versions, it's not your fault. It's their fault. Also, it's considered hip these days for a company to send direct mail to its installed base. By registering, you're going to get junk mail, but some junk mail contains great bargains.

Try the simple things first. Getting technical support, even from the best companies, is a pain in the bus. Avoid it as much as possible by trying the simple things before you call. Rebuild your desktop by restarting your

Macintosh while holding down the Option and Command keys. Reinstall the software from the original disks that you bought, because applications and their adjunct files get corrupted. You might as well try these things before you call, because the support person is going to ask you to do them anyway.

Know what you've got. If the simple things don't work, make sure that you know what you have in your system *before* you call. Start by finding out the version of the software you're using. To do this, choose the About command from the Apple menu. This provides a dialog box with version information.

Also, know what kinds of INITs and control panels you're running, because a favorite cop-out for companies is to blame the vagaries of INIT and control panel conflicts. This is a manifestation of bozo support: "Avoid solving a customer's problem, make the customer think he did something wrong, and send him off to look for his own solution."

The way to avoid this is to know in advance what's in your system. You can do this by running a program such as Profiler (part of Now Software's Now Utilities) or the freeware program TattleTale, which has similar abilities. These products provide a report of what's running in your system.

Then when a support person says, "This sounds like an INIT (or control panel) conflict," you say, "What INITs (or control panels) cause this? I know exactly what I have in my system." You are permitted to think, "Make my day, bozo."

See if you can duplicate the problem. The most frustrating problems for both users and support people are problems that can't be repeated. Before you call, try to make the problem repeat itself. Record exactly what you've done. This provides useful clues to support people to figure out what's gone wrong. If you can't make a problem repeat, go to the next paragraph.

Get a life. Many people who call for technical support are victims of self-inflicted abuse: "When I'm in Excel with Talking Moose turned on but not talking, right after After Dark launches the flying toaster screen saver if I hold down the tab, shift, option, and delete key and launch About Excel with my Radius Pivot in landscape mode, I crash. Is there a fix for this?"

There is a fix: don't do it. To paraphrase Goodman Ace, if something hurts when you do it, don't do it. Sometimes support people are justified in telling callers, "This sounds like an INIT conflict."

When You Call

Be sly. A trick to getting through to a company's technical support people is to figure out their biorhythms. Some people like to start early and get a jump on the day. Some like to work late, because they don't have lives. Some like to work during lunch, because customers don't call during lunch, because they think that the support people are out. Experiment until you figure out the best time to call.

Always make progress. Some people take lithium before they call companies with voice mail and message-taking devices. They're wrong. These tools are a terrific aid to support if you remember one thing: Always make progress. Don't leave a message like, "This is Steve Jobs I have a problem. Call me back at (408) 555-1010."

Instead leave a message like this: "This is Steve Jobs. I am using version 4.01 of WordMaker running under System

7.0.1 on my IIci with 8 megabytes of RAM running at 16 shades of gray. I crash when I try to add more columns to an existing table. Please call me back at (408) 555-1010 until 6:00 pm PST. From 6:00 to 6:30 I'll be in my car; the car phone number is (408) 555-2227. After 6:30 I'll be home at (408) 555-2393."

Be succinct. On the other hand, don't be verbose. Provide the pertinent information to solve your problem. Don't waste time with an essay about why they should help you: "I bought my first copy of your software when it was running on an Apple II. Since then, I've bought two more copies. I tell my friends to buy it. Once, I was at a user group meeting and a salesman from your company did a demo. I think his name was Biff, or maybe Bruce. I thought his demo was lousy."

Develop a close relationship. The voice at the other end of the line is a person. A human being with hopes, aspirations, dreams, desires, and frustrations. Rather than treating that person as your butler, concierge, or slave, foster a relationship. Latch onto one person and write down his or her name and extension so that you get person-to-person support instead of a party line.

Here are the best ways: Write to the person's supervisor and say what a great job the person is doing, send him a gift, or send a sample of your company's products. Over the course of several years, grateful customers have sent me books, Danish pastries, steaks, pork chops, t-shirts, footballs, and one of every computer product that 3M ever made for customers. My favorite gift of all time, though— what with my being a wife and all—was a box of Dow Chemical household products.

If All Else Fails

If none of these techniques yeilds satisfactory support, then my suggestion is that you contact the president of the company. This is an art in itself.

Send a Fax. Faxes are hip. In the evolution of business correspondence, first people sent letters to get attention, then they made telephone calls, then they sent letters via Federal Express. Now they send faxes. There's something about a fax that makes it seem urgent.

Start Your Fax on a Positive Note. Honey, sugar, even Nutrasweet works better than vinegar. Start your fax with a sentence like this: "I enjoy using your product. It is among my favorite applications. Frankly, I consider it justification to buy a Macintosh."

State Your Problem Succinctly. Do not send a fax that is longer than one page (two, counting the cover page). State your problem, and ask for resolution. Nobody wants to hear your entire woeful plight.

Don't (Try to) Get an Employee in Trouble. There's a high probability that the person you try to skewer is the one who is assigned to help you. Describe everyone's effort, regardless of what happened, like this: "Jane has been extremely helpful and professional, but we still haven't completely resolved the problem."

If writing to the president fails, then it's time to vote with your feet and your dollars. Some companies and customers were just not meant to build a relationship with each other. That's okay—just move on. And if you find you have a compelling need to write to a columnist about your experience, I suggest Debra Branscum at *Macworld*. Leave me alone.[1]

[1] I regreted writing the last sentence. People thought, correctly, that I was being a jerk by telling my readers not to bug me. But if you could see some of the letters I got, you'd know why I was getting ragged. On the other hand, I was a hero to every tech support person in the industry, and now I get amazing tech support when I call.

user group Software pirates gone legit.

Undo Bringing Steve Jobs back to Apple.

undocumented feature A bug in your company's software. See also *bug*.

unexpected result A bug in your company's software. See also *bug*.

UNIX Emasculated system software that doesn't use a pointing device.

update Revising software to get comarketing from Apple and distributing it for free.

upgrade Revising software to get comarketing from Apple and charging for it.

upwardly compatible A rich spouse who lets you connect to CompuServe at night.

user group Software pirates gone legit.

People wearing ties do lousy user-group demos.

For every software pirate in a user group, there are ten personal computer administrators from Fortune 1,000 companies.

user interface Whatever Alan Kay says it is.

"People wearing ties do lousy user-group demos."

venture capitalist A person who made money because of luck, but is convinced it was because of brains.

VAR Very Aggravating Reseller.

venture capitalist A person who made money because of luck, but is convinced it was because of brains.

> *Luck is the factor most highly correlated with a successful venture capitalist.*

For still more on venture capital, see "Don't Kvetch, Kick Butt," at the end of this chapter.

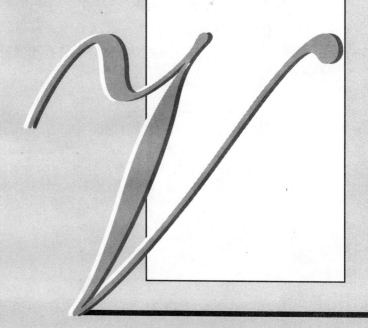

virtual memory A System 7 feature that makes it almost possible to run software with slightly more memory than you have.[1]

virtual reality Really good PR.

*"The difference
between
advertising and
PR is advertis-
ing is when you
say you're good
and PR is when
others say
you're good. PR
is better."*

> *"The difference between advertising and PR is advertising is when you say you're good and PR is when others say you're good. PR is better."* (Told to me by Jean-Louis Gassée during one of his tortuously long and unproductive Monday morning staff meetings.)

virus A marketing ploy to sell more utilities.

More on venture capital (or lack of it)...

Don't Kvetch, Kick Butt

Reprinted from *MacUser* March 1991

Software developers are in a tizzy these days. One half complains about how hard it is to penetrate the Mac market. The other half believes that the Macintosh market isn't worth penetrating, so they're going to Windows.

I don't agree with either half, but I care only about the first half. The second half can go to Hell. This column is about ways in which small Macintosh software companies can penetrate the Macintosh market—even today. It's also my own small contribution to helping break Microsoft's stranglehold on personal computing.

[1] Thanks to Matt Evens

The Press

Principle: Dealing with the press takes a rifle, not a shotgun, approach. There are only three publications—*MacUser*, *Macworld*, and *MacWEEK*—that developers have to worry about. (Maybe I should add *InfoWorld*, but its Macintosh coverage centers on proving that Windows will kill the Mac.)

The revelation that there are only three publications to cover has enormous impact. It means that developers don't need to spend $25,000 on a party to impress 200 champagne-guzzlers.

Three editors—Russ Ito of *MacUser*, Carol Person of *Macworld*, and Henry Norr of *MacWEEK*—are the most important press contacts developers can make. The best way to get to them is to call them and show them a product. This might cost a developer a trip to the Bay Area and three lunches. (Henry Norr's favorite place to eat is the Rinconada Center.)

Although these three people are the most important, they focus on new product announcements and reviews. There are other editors and writers who do lab-based comparison articles, feature stories, tips-and-tricks columns, and end-user profiles. The best strategy is to find a product champion from among the editors and writers by sending a copy of the product to every person on a magazine's masthead.

A personalized cover letter, press release, and the name of the company contact should accompany the product. After developers send their products, they should follow up by calling each recipient. Many developers think that the box of software the postman dumps off will blow editors away so much that they will be compelled to write a story or column about it. Dream on. I haven't opened most of the software I've received this way.

Distributors

Principle: A product gets the level of distribution it deserves. Large, successful software companies who want to gobble up developers ("acquire your product") and high-priced marketing consultants would have developers believe that "distribution is impossible to get these days." Hogwash. It's not impossible if a developer has a hot product. Let me explain.

Products such as PageMaker, Word, and Excel are commodity items. Every distributor (a distributor buys products from developers and resells them to dealers) has to carry them, and this means that everyone competes on price. Hot new products are not commodity items, so for awhile, distributors and dealers can make a lot of money on them. Thus, a product can be desirable even if it's not from a big vendor.

Just as there are only a handful of magazines, there are a handful of distributors that matter. Really, there are only two: MacAmerica and Ingram/Micro D. So developers only have to impress two people: MacAmerica's Jack Koll and Ingram/Micro D's Sue Harvey.

The same rifle approach works on distributors: call them up, tell them about the product, and go show it to them. Believe me, if a product is hot, they will fall over themselves trying to acquire it.

Dealers

Principle: Concentrate on end-user pull, not on dealer push. Should developers try to go crazy and find, recruit, and train 3,000 dealers around the world? No way. Dealers sell the products that people ask for at their particular store. A developer's job is to generate crowds of people who come in asking for its products.

Frankly, most developers don't get dealer shelf space because dealers have very little shelf space to give. This is OK, because most Macintosh software is sold through mail-order companies anyway. If developers can convince MacConnection, MacWarehouse, and MacAvenue to carry their products, their distribution is set. If developers can get Egghead, then distribution is truly done and they can concentrate on generating demand.

Before I antagonize every dealer, I would like to mention that there are a handful of stores that set the trend for the nation. They include ComputerWare in the San Francisco Bay Area; North Shore Computers in Milwaukee, Wisconsin; MacEmporium in New York City; and MacUniverse in Los Angeles, California.

ComputerWare in particular is a good test: if ComputerWare can't sell your product, no other dealer will be able to. The cheapest market research a developer can buy is to call up the Palo Alto store and ask for Yuji Honma. If he thinks your product will sell, it will sell.

User Groups

Principle: Help friends first. If you've been reading my column for a while, you know I love user groups. There's something very touching about people who band together to improve people's Macintosh computing experience without any monetary compensation.

These groups are developers' friends. One of their primary purposes is to disseminate information—and developers have information—about their new products. This is a perfect match, yet most developers do not work user groups. Many developers think that user groups are a bunch of crabby people who sit around complaining. In fact user groups are a medium more powerful than most Macintosh magazines.

Therefore, developers need to get off their derriere and work with user groups. Every developer should send every Macintosh user group a review copy of the product; 50 brochures and flyers; and a free perpetual subscription to any company newsletter about the product. One more thing: every developer should visit every major user group to do a demo at least once per year.

I'll put my money where my mouth is. If you want a database of the kinds of Mac contacts that I mentioned, contact me and I'll send you a copy. It's for the common good. Get out there; kick some butt. The whole Macintosh community will love you for it.

wimp Anyone who backs up his or her hard disk.

warranty The time period during which your computer does not break.

> *A Macintosh will break when you open the box, or on the 366th day.*

> *Apple employees will tell you they have never heard of what your Macintosh did.*

> *Dealer employees will tell you that what your Macintosh did happens all the time.*

wide area network Any network too large for LocalTalk.

"Never take your PowerBook and your wife on the same vacation."

widow   The spouse of a computer owner.

wife   A person—male or female—who doubles the time it takes to write a software program (or book) and then asks why the royalties take so long to arrive.

> *Never take your PowerBook and your wife on the same vacation.*

wimp   Anyone who backs up his or her hard disk.

Windows   Software that makes a 80386 run as slow as a 68000.

More on Windows...

Windows Hell

A Microsoft Windows programmer died, and he went to where the Committee decides whether a person goes to Heaven or Hell.

The Committee asked the programmer if he wanted to see Heaven and Hell before he made his choice. "Sure," he said, so an angel guided him to a place where there was a sunny beach, volleyball, rock 'n roll, and where everyone was having a great time. "Wow!" he exclaimed. "That was great! Was that Heaven?"

"Nope," said the angel. "That was Hell. Want to see Heaven?"

"Sure!" So the angel took him to another place. This time there were a bunch of people sitting in a park playing bingo and feeding dead pigeons.

"This is Heaven?" asked the Windows programmer.

"Yup," said the angel.

"I'll take Hell," he said without hesitation. And instantly he found himself immersed in seething volcanic lava with his clothes and hair being burnt from his body.

"Where's the beach? The music? The volleyball?" he screamed frantically as the heat began to overcome him.

"That was the demo," replied the angel as he vanished.

---

workstation A computer with a powerful processor, ugly interface, and no software.

write-protect Advertising in a magazine to ensure a good review.

WYSIWYG When You Ship Is When You Get. A compensation and bonus plan for programmers.

More on wives...

My Life as a Wife

Reprinted from *MacUser* October 1991

Copyright © 1991, Ziff Communications Company

I have a lot of free time these days. I never had this much free time because I was always one of those DOs (diligent orientals) obsessed with overachievement. You know the kind: takes advanced-placement courses in high school, graduates early from college, gets an M.B.A. while working full time, slaves at Apple, and starts a company.

I'm off the fast track now, because I realized that all men are cremated equal. What's the use of killing yourself as a corporate slave? Instead, I'm concentrating on leaving the best-looking corpse I can, and I'm also turning into a wife. This column is about what it's like to be a Macintosh wife.

You can be a Macintosh wife whether you're a man or a woman. I'm not being sexist, just empirically accurate. If this offends you, I'll send you the file for this column and you can substitute "hife" or "wusband" to make yourself happy. The point of this column is for you to appreciate your wife. You probably think that your life is hard, and your wife's life is easy.

Parameter-RAM Caching

Be forewarned: this column has almost nothing to do with Macintosh. If you don't like it, I'm sure there's a feature story comparing parameter-RAM caching in the top 100 3 1/2-inch hard disks somewhere in this issue. Also, if you're the wife of a Microsoft employee who emigrated from Singapore to search for political freedom, who likes to keep a machine gun around the house in case a herd of deer attacks, you'll probably dislike this column.

While you're at work mousing around, reading *MacWEEK*, pondering the impact of System 7 on INITs, and trying to stop Microsoft Word from unexpectedly quitting, we wives are at home suffering. You probably think that it's easy to keep a home and family running compared to the stress of shipping a faster version of software and making sure that there's lots of software for a computer with 128K of RAM from a company whose role model seems to be a Latin American dictatorship. You're wrong.

It's not easy. Here are three reasons why. First, there is no support structure. At work, there are receptionists; secretaries; shipping clerks; and, God help us, management. At home, you face each crisis, no matter how small it may seem, all alone. Second, there is no camaraderie. At work, you can wander over to the next cubicle to bounce ideas off colleagues or to commiserate. At home, there isn't a next cubicle at all. Frankly, it's often quite lonely being a wife. Third, there is little tangible feedback. At work, there are milestones such as finishing a project, shipping a product, and getting a performance review. At home, each day seems like the day before, and I doubt that most couples get together to review their performance.

The Gory Details

So that you may gain a greater appreciation of what it's like to be a wife, let me provide a tongue-in-cheek description of a wife's life. I'm explicitly telling you that it's tongue in cheek because the minds of some readers are so fragmented that they can't tell when I'm kidding.

Eating a meal becomes an event. Eating takes on enormous importance—almost as much as reading E-mail—because it breaks your day into pieces: breakfast, before lunch, lunch, before dinner, dinner, and before breakfast. If you're a '90s wife like me, half of your meals are eaten at restaurants. (You'll know that eating is becoming important when you stop caring about the speed of service. From my perspective, I have to read the *San Jose Mercury News*, *San Francisco Chronicle*, and *The Wall Street Journal* anyway. I force myself to read *The Wall Street Journal* so that I can relate to my spouse's career.)

Because eating takes on such significance, so does exercising. Arnold Schwartznegger would be proud: I lift weights two times a week and play basketball three times a week. The high point of lifting weights is often seeing other professional athletes—like Roger Craig, Jerry Rice, and Ronnie Lott—working out at the same time. It's kind of a male bonding thing that transcends wifedom. The high point of playing basketball is watching the others hurry back to work without having lunch. I haven't gotten into aerobics yet, because I hate putting on makeup and crotch-floss outfits to work out.

Shop Till You Drop

Getting back to eating, you really *shop* for food. Shopping for food used to mean buying Jolt at Seven Eleven. It was GIGO shopping: Get In and Get Out. Now shopping for food takes on the significance of an offsite retreat; it means going to multiple markets based on their relative strengths. For example, when I make pot roast, I go to one market to buy a specific onion soup mix. Then I make another trip to another market to buy a specific kind of meat. I once saw Steve Jobs at this market, and he told me, "If you ever want to do something important with your life again, contact me."

When you're a wife, you also really *cook* food. Cooking food used to mean opening the aforementioned Jolt and calling for a pizza. Not when you're a wife; when you're a wife, you cook from scratch because it uses up time and because it makes you feel like you're contributing to the happiness of your (working) spouse. I love to have a hot meal waiting at home for my spouse when she gets home from work. It really disappoints me when she gets home late, and the food is cold. Later in the column, I'm going to provide my heretofore secret recipe for teriyaki chicken.

Pick-a-Little, Talk-a-Little

You hang around with other wives. My circle of daytime friends has changed from the likes of Randy Battat (a vice president at Apple) to his wife, Chris, and her two Portables: Scott and Alexandra. We always bump into each other at the market or at the mall. When we bump into each other, we always ask the obligatory questions: "How is Randy/Beth doing at work?" "Are you thinking of going back to work soon?" (Answer: I'm taking some part-time work, but Randy/Beth really wants me to stay at home with Portables.") I've heard from other wives— particularly the ones who used to be hotshot business executives—that there is no substitute for raising Portables. Nothing, it seems, could be more important or more satisfying than raising Portables.

You learn a lot of strategic things about running a home. Here are six. First, laundry that's been washed can stay in the washer for two days before it starts smelling bad and you have to wash it again. Second, laundry that has been dried can stay in the drier as long as your spouse doesn't need clothes. Third, putting water into dirty dishes and pots reduces the effort to wash the dishes and pots by 80 percent. Fourth, 20 percent of the dishes account for 80 percent of the usage. (Pareto's law of dishes). With proper selection, you never have to put dishes away. Fifth, you cannot go to Price Club without spending at least $200. (This is a very good omen for selling Classics in superstores.) Sixth, a great deal of Price Club merchandise can fit into a Porsche 911.

You try to talk a lot to your spouse when he or she gets home. After being bored all day, you need to talk to an intelligent human being about something other than the rising cost of groceries. I always ask my spouse about her day so that I can live through her vicariously: "I met with the agency people from Foote, Cone, & Belding. We discussed the new ads we're shooting with Spike Lee. My ad budget has been increased to $25 million. How was your day?" I worked out and then had a cafe mocha then went marketing (*food* marketing, not strategic, "Helocar" marketing).

Finger Lickin' Teriyaki Chicken

You may not have noticed, but I try to write columns that provide information that my readers can use. This month, instead of tips on how to use PageMaker or Photoshop better, I'm going to provide my world-famous teriyaki chicken recipe. Ingredients: two pounds of assorted chicken parts, two cups of high-sodium soy sauce, two cups of sugar, one cup of chopped green onions, two tablespoons of minced ginger, two minced jalapeño peppers, and two tablespoons of sesame seed oil.

Directions: combine all the ingredients except the chicken. Mix well (I use the Cuisinart that Jean-Louis gave us for our wedding gift). Add the chicken and let it all marinate for two to three hours. Remove the mixture and microwave for 15 minutes at the highest temperature setting. Barbecue it to complete cooking and to add color to the skin. The chicken is done when the flesh starts to pull away from the knuckles of the bones.

Sick of Stacks

Some of you may contact me because you are sympathetic to my need for a career. Some of you will even send me HyperCard stacks that you think are the next Lotus 1-2-3 (the PC version, not the Macintosh version). Save your disks, because I like being a wife as much as I hate looking at HyperCard stacks.

On the other hand, you could send me your favorite recipe (but please don't send me any software to keep track of recipes). The most important thing for you to do, however, is to tell your wife how much you appreciate him or her. I've got to go… it's time for basketball and then lunch and then marketing.[1]

---

[1]This was my favorite of all the columns I wrote for *MacUser*. It generated the most response of all my columns. To my surprise and relief, many women loved it. I also received about twenty-five recipes.

Zodiac I don't have a definition for "Zodiac," but I wanted to maintain parallel structure, so this "definition" is here. I am a Virgo, and Virgos are meticulous.

X-modem Choosing your spouse instead of E-mail.

XCMD A computer executive's former company.

Y-modem Explaining why your E-mail bill is large.

zealotry That which makes you believe before you see.

For still more on zealotry, see "Praise the Macintosh," at the end of this chapter.

Zodiac I don't have a definition for "Zodiac," but I wanted to maintain parallel structure, so this "definition" is here. I am a Virgo, and Virgos are meticulous.

More on Zodiacs...

The Macintosh Zodiac

Aries Aries Macintosh owners seek challenge and change. For them each new version of System 7 and Microsoft Word is a thrill. Independent and tough minded, Aries Macintosh owners hate to share printers or modems. They are among the few people who believe in the future of multimedia. Favorite application: Macromind Director.

Taurus Taurus Macintosh owners are tenacious and need to possess and control their computers. They are not content to accept explanations like "There's an INIT conflict," or "It's a bug in System 7." At times dogmatic, they may argue with software companies about how software should work. Favorite application: 4th Dimension.

Gemini Gemini Macintosh owners are creative, refreshing, and artsy-fartsy. They frequently change their desktop patterns and pictures and screen savers. Since Gemini is ruled by Mercury, the messenger of the gods, Gemini Macintosh owners are often E-mail addicts. Favorite application: More After Dark.

Cancer Cancer Macintosh owners are emotional, dramatic, and imaginative. They become too attached to files and hence always run out of disk space. They are as likely to be in love with their Macintoshes as wanting to cut them in half with a chainsaw—but never in between. Favorite application: Adobe Photoshop.

Leo Leo Macintosh owners are kind, generous, and happy. They believe that Apple will always provide upgrade paths and bug fixes. They do, however, have a need to dominate and be in the limelight, so they tend to buy the latest software and assume the bugs will be worked out. Favorite application: WordPerfect.

Virgo Virgo Macintosh owners are workaholics, meticulous and hypochondriacal. They rebuild their desktop and defragment their hard disks at least once a week. They are completely honest, so they never accept pirated software, and they always pay for the shareware that they use. Favorite application: DiskExpress II.

Libra Libra Macintosh owners believe in justice, orderliness, and morality. They often strive for harmony in their computing space—cheerfully resolving what others would consider problems such as INIT and font conflicts. When a user group crowd skewers a demonstrator, Libras leap to the demonstrator's defense. Favorite application: Startup Manager (Now Software).

Scorpio Scorpio Macintosh owners are fascinated (and at times obsessed) with power. They are persistent, determined, and strong willed—willing to spend weeks to master an application. These qualities can turn into obsessive relationships with certain pieces of software. Favorite application: HyperCard.

Sagittarius Sagittarius Macintosh owners are perpetual motion machines full of energy, a sense of adventure, and intuitive insights. Of all Macintosh owners, they have the most applications—often owning more than one product in a category. This makes Sagittarius owners the delight of software companies. Favorite application: MultiFinder.

Capricorn Capricorn Macintosh owners are loyal survivors who have stuck with Apple. Many of them owned an Apple II, upgraded to a IIgs, and even bought the Apple II card for their LC. Though solidly grounded, Capricorn Macintosh owners are sometimes drawn to drama—for

More on Zodiacs . . . **195**

example, considering the purchase of a NeXT machine, so that they can be loyal to Steve again. Favorite application: AppleWorks.

Aquarius Aquarius Macintosh owners are the Macintosh equivalent of hippies from *Hair*. They long for a world of fair, open, and natural Macintosh computing, free of copy protection, installer disks, and compression utilities. They despise products from companies whose executives drive nice cars. Favorite application: KidPix, version 1.0 (the shareware version).

---

zoom rectangles Proof that Microsoft went beyond the license it got from Apple.

More on zealotry...

Praise the Macintosh

Reprinted from *MacUser* August 1990

Back when I worked for Apple, my job title was software evangelist. Full of fervor and zeal, I would meet with developers, show them a Macintosh prototype, and convince them to develop Macintosh software. I thought I knew a lot about evangelism.

I learned something recently: There are a lot of people who know a lot more about evangelism than I do. This revelation occurred when I attended the Billy Graham School of Evangelism in Albany, New York, last April. This was a four-day course in evangelism for pastors and ministers. (If you're wondering why I went, it was because

I'm writing a book about evangelism.) Let me share this experience with you.

Not the Center of the Universe

I arrived in Albany after attending the 1990 National Apple User Group Conference. It was quite a transition to go from a conference where people talked only about Macintosh to a conference where people had barely heard of it. For a while, I was in a state of shock. My wife attributes this to the extensive ego damage that occurred because no one at the conference knew who I was.

One thing I could immediately relate to was the quantity of books for sale near the registration desk. Arthur Naiman of *Macintosh Bible* fame would die and go to heaven if he knew how many books were sold over the course of four days. I know I did.

Fish Out of Water

I was clearly a fish out of water at the conference. Attending was not the equivalent of a Macintosh owner going to Macworld Expo. It was the equivalent of a humble Macintosh owner going to a hackers-only event, such as the Apple Developer's Conference. Ministers and pastors are different from you and me. For example, when we sang hymns, everyone knew them by heart. Except me. I just hummed softly a lot.

For example, when the instructors said, "Let's read X passage together," everyone opened their Bibles directly to the passage. It's called DBA (Direct Bible Access). I had to develop another technique: "Hmm, he's about two-thirds of the way into his Bible. I'll start looking from about two-thirds through mine." After a while, I just pretended to be taking copious notes.

For example, I learned that it's perfectly OK to shout out "Praise the Lord" or "Amen" in the middle of a presentation. One woman shouted "Praise the Lord" every two minutes. I thought she was rude, but I guess I was wrong, because she was publicly introduced on the last day. If she were a member of BMUG, she would be the one at the meetings shouting "Praise the Macintosh."

Conference Camaraderie

The attendees showed an incredible level of camaraderie and friendliness—much more than those at Macworld Expo or Apple Developer's Conference attendees. I made two buddies on the first day—two guys from New Hampshire called Hank and Dick. Hank was a retiree who wanted to join a pastoral staff. Dick refurbished submarines during the week and was a pastor on weekends.

After we got into his 1970 Cadillac, Dick said, "Don't let the car fool you; we're as poor as Job." As we were driving around looking for the conference hotel, Dick said to Hank and me, "I'll drive, you navigate, and this guy will pray." We *did* find the place in a very short time.

On Believing

If you think that Macintosh owners believe, ministers and pastors *believe*. And they don't complain—about bugs in the world or about when the second coming will ship. They also *believe* in prayer. If they prayed just once for System 7, it would ship, bug-free, before the Boston Macworld Expo (the August 1990 one, that is).

Our industry could learn a lot by going to a conference such as this. Admittedly, you have to get past the singing, the praying, the holding hands, and the arm waving and approach it with an open mind. Once you do, however, there is more solid marketing information than at the conferences I usually attend. For example, one session explained how to make good speeches. It covered background preparation, the qualities of an effective message, delivery of the message, and how to invite response.

We could also learn a lot about how to put on a conference. Every session started and ended on time. Each attendee was given a syllabus that contained the outlines of every presentation. (Have you ever gotten a syllabus for a Macworld Expo or Apple Developer's Conference presentation?) And to top it all off, the four-day conference cost $25 and you could get a scholarship if you couldn't afford it. Twenty-five bucks barely gets you a hot dog and a Coke at Macworld Expo.

Outstanding Speakers

The speakers at the conference were outstanding. Apple should hire them to introduce its new computers. Every opening joke worked. Every speech was peppered with great stories, analogies, and metaphors. The speakers "built" the presentations: "There are four key points to discipling. Point 1 is.... Point 2 is.... Point 3 is.... Point 4 is.... " Frankly, the worst speaker at the conference (and I would be hard-pressed to pick a bad speaker) was about three times better than the best speaker in the computer business.

I tried to illustrate this to Dick one night during dinner at Denny's: "The plenary-session speaker was a much better speaker than John Sculley." His response was, "Who's John Sculley?" I didn't bother comparing the speaker to Jean-Louis: "Well, you see, there was this French guy with a diamond earring who was president of one-fourth of

Apple until he told *The Wall Street Journal* he was going to resign because Apple had brought in this German guy who also used to run one-fourth of Apple...."

All in all, I'm glad I went. I learned a lot about evangelism. I learned a lot about Christianity. And I met some very nice people. I'm going to see them again when I'm in Boston for Macworld Expo. Maybe, I'll bring them to the Expo and show them the Macintosh way. A good evangelist never rests.